THE

BADASS

LADIES'

GUIDE

TO

EMBRACING

POSSIBILITY

DITCH YOUR NEGATIVE THOUGHTS
AND GET OUT OF YOUR
OWN WAY

OLIVIA KIMBLE

CONTENTS

"When a woman rises up in glory, her energy is magnetic and her sense of possibility contagious" - Marianne Williamson

INTRODUCTION: WHY BOTHER?

You're feeling stuck. Maybe you've been barely getting by for a long time, secretly feeling unfulfilled and unhappy. You might be making choices that don't feel right or feel like you don't have a choice at all.

Sound familiar?

It was familiar for me, too. I wasted so much time being stuck because I felt like I *couldn't* make any other choices. I was bogged down by everyone's expectations and opinions. I stopped caring what I thought and thought only of what other people would think of me.

The thing is, I was doing fine. I made it through every day, got home, and watched TV. You're probably the same way. You know on some subconscious level that you're capable of more, but things are okay right now.

Why bother making all that effort to change?

First off, I'm not here to tell you that you need to change. I think that's something you're already thinking about, or you wouldn't have picked up this book. I *am* here to show you how you're holding yourself back, so you can decide if change is what you need. I'm sure you've got enough people trying to tell you what to do!

If you feel trapped by your thoughts and feelings, the changes in this book will help you move through that. Maybe you feel frustrated with your circumstances and keep thinking about what could've been. It's so easy to be angry at the world. You might feel betrayed because you did everything right and still got screwed by the system. It isn't your fault, and let's be real: It sucks.

But what does it feel like to hold on to all that anger? Is it helping you?

Maybe it gives you a barrier that protects you from the world because no one is going to mess with the woman who looks like she wants to kick your ass. In a weird way, it can be comforting to walk around knowing that no one is really seeing you. Your feelings and the fragile, soft parts of you are safe inside that hard shell.

Unfortunately, it also keeps you from making real connections with people. You might miss out on opportunities for close, loving friendships because you can't open up. You always have to keep that mask on.

This cycle can even keep you from making progress at work. You can end up in the completely wrong career—almost by accident. Your real dreams can feel out of reach. You can be wildly successful and still feel completely unfulfilled if that success doesn't mean anything to you.

So, even if the world is screwing you over, you're making it worse by backing it up. You feel like you can't change anything, so you let the world trample you. You don't have to feel powerless or stuck. It'll be hard to get out of that feeling, but you can do it, and you don't have to do it alone.

In this book, we'll cover exactly what you're doing to hold yourself back, including what you say and believe about yourself and the world. You might think that having a negative voice in your head keeps you from overstepping or getting full of yourself, but it has way more impact than that.

You'll learn the psychology behind all these little things, why they keep you stuck, and how to stop doing them. We'll even dig into your past to figure out where these feelings came from, so you can better understand yourself (and stop doing that!).

The way you think about yourself can even change your body, and vice versa. So, if you've been feeling crappy, that might be why! You'll figure out how to take better care of both your body and mind, and it isn't what you think. This isn't another broken record telling you to eat better and go to the gym. You have my word!

After that, we'll get into the way you handle friendships and relationships. Your daily habits could be making you lonelier and more stressed. I'll help you tease apart what you're doing and how to stop doing it.

Part of that process is shutting up the critical voice in your head. You'll learn how to do some good old-fashioned self-care, too. No, it doesn't always involve bubble baths or face masks (sorry)!

Then, it's time to explore. You'll start to see that there are way more options in your life than you thought possible. You don't have to change your whole life to see the difference; you just have to try a few new things. Once you get there, you'll be ready to delve into your passions and start writing the future you want.

That might sound overwhelming or like it's not going to happen, and I get that.

If it doesn't work for you, you can quit at any moment. What's the harm in at least giving it a try?

If you start to get overwhelmed at any point, just flip to Chapter 10. You'll find a whole chapter on all the most common problems women encounter as they go through this process. Everyone gets to that point at least once during any major life change, so you should never feel like you're failing. It's totally normal!

Finally, you'll learn how to tell if you've made it. When you make small changes over time, you might feel like you aren't really that different from when you began. But, when you look at the big picture, you can more clearly see how far you've come.

As a sneak peek, going through this process will help you spend more time on stuff you enjoy, not just vegging out in front of the TV. Plus, it will improve your relationships and help you truly feel better. What's not to like?

Every step in this book is grounded in real psychology, so you'll know you're on the right track.

If you feel like this is all too much work, that's okay. You don't have to do it all at once, and these pages are still going to be here when you're ready to take the next step.

You have more power than you think, and you can live the life you want.

After all, you're a badass, and you know what that means? Here's my favorite definition:

She's a strong, confident, bold woman who knows her own mind. She is sexy, she is funny, she knows what she wants, and she doesn't need anyone's approval. Being a badass is about knowing your own worth and not letting anyone else mess with that. It's about taking control and becoming the best version of yourself. (Cleave, 2021)

I *know* that's who you are deep down, and I want you to embrace that!

You're powerful, smart, and a force to be reckoned with.

Use that power to become the truest version of yourself.

YOUR PERSONAL BRAND OF BADASS

If you've read this far, you know one thing for sure: Something doesn't feel quite right about where you're at right now. What feels wrong will depend on who you are and what stage you're at in your life. It could be something big and obvious that you already know needs to change... or it might be a few small things that you can't quite put your finger on.

Whether you know where the feeling is coming from or not, it's easy to get overwhelmed by it. That feeling of "wrongness" can keep you up at night. It might haunt every moment of your day in some small way. Or you could be drowning it in distracting activities that don't really fulfill you. It's time to stop letting those feelings control your life!

That's what being a badass really boils down to, after all: It's knowing what invigorates, excites, and fulfills you, and refusing to compromise on your own happiness.

For most people, becoming your most badass self involves some kind of movement. You're moving toward the things that make life feel exciting and worthwhile and away from the things that don't.

At first, it can be hard to figure out what those things are. We have lots of little habits that are part of our routine but don't give us much joy or satisfaction. Still, they're part of our day, and it's hard to even think about replacing them.

Start thinking about what you might want to change in your life. It might just be a few small things or maybe just a feeling. Maybe you don't really want to change what you do, but you still want to approach your life with more confidence.

STARTING SMALL

No matter where you're starting from, it's okay to be where you are. It's okay to be in a rut, to feel down, to be confused, unsure, or looking for a missing piece. Every day is a chance to begin again, and that starts with being kind to yourself and honoring where you're coming from. There's nothing wrong with you. Read that again: *There's nothing wrong with you!*

To start changing your life in a healthy way, you need to begin with love. I know, I know: gross. But having some compassion for where you're at is key to starting your journey on the right foot.

You probably can't train to climb Mount Everest if you've got five kids running around! That doesn't mean you shouldn't dream big, but you *should* take inventory of what stage you're at in your life. We tend to imagine that everyone does all these big, fun things in their early 20s: goes to college, settles down, has kids, and works a day job until they retire. Maybe that's how your life has been going... but maybe that just isn't for you!

For example, my coach started off his 30s at 300 pounds and went on to become a triathlete at the national level! At the beginning, he decided to join because he loved to run, cycle, and swim. All he wanted was to finish the race. When he did, it was a huge accomplishment. He kept doing the races just for fun as a way to keep fit and constantly improve.

He improved way more than he could ever have imagined. He got noticed by coaches who convinced him that he was capable of even more.

My coach didn't start off with a huge dream. If he had, he might've been too intimidated to even start. He started small and just worked on improving at something he cared about. Finally, when a coach approached him, he was open to his own capabilities. He could've turned down the coach, believing that he wasn't able to do any more. Instead, he fought through his own doubts to achieve something truly amazing.

Not everyone lives their life in strict stages. There's no reason that you can't have fun life adventures in your 30s, 60s, or even after that! Don't give in to the pressure to do what's "normal" if that doesn't work for you. You're the one driving this life, and you get to choose which roads you take!

So, if you're in a situation where your big dream isn't possible yet, you shouldn't give up on it. Just plan ahead for it! Chances are that there are small things you can do today to plan for that big dream. Don't psych yourself out by worrying about the big picture yet. Just see where you're at and take a baby step forward from there.

Speaking of, let's dive into some different possibilities, so you can figure out what you want to work toward.

FINANCIAL FREEDOM

For many women, the ultimate way to embrace their inner badass is to be financially independent, running their own business, and make money their own way. This is an awesome dream, but it's also a big one!

If you've got a big business idea, then this could be an exciting direction for you. There are lots of steps that would need to fall into place, but you can plan out those steps in later chapters so that you're totally ready for it. If that's your big dream, you should honor it! Just remember to break your dream into smaller pieces, so it doesn't feel overwhelming.

The thing is that you don't need to run your own company to become financially free. For many of us, that kind of a risk is not just scary but totally out of the question. If that's you, you can still find your own way to financial freedom.

Alternatively, you might want to find a job that makes you happier, or ask for a raise so that bills are less stressful. Finding a position that makes you feel valued and respected can take a lot of patience and effort. Maybe searching for a fun job with great pay is the next big step for you. Or, maybe for you, financial freedom is about letting yourself spend a little extra cash on yourself (not just on the kids or your friends).

See what I mean? You don't have to take a giant leap of faith to make lasting, meaningful change. You just have to commit to a small change that will push you in the direction you want to go.

BODY FREEDOM

Do you feel like your body is holding you back from becoming your most badass self? Maybe physical limitations literally keep you from activities you love. Or maybe poor self-esteem is making you too embarrassed or afraid to try things you'd love to do. Maybe you'd like to get in better shape, so you can do more things with your family.

Depending on where you're at, achieving bodily freedom might be about moving your body every single day. Maybe you need to buckle down and really make a commitment to yourself, so you can finally live the life you've been dreaming about.

For others, that might not be an option. Your body freedom might be about finding creative ways to enjoy activities you love without putting yourself at risk. If you're a person with a physical

4

limitation, you might look up how people in your circumstances have done the activity that you want to do. Chances are that someone has found a way to make it work!

If that isn't possible, you can always look for a compromise. How can you honor your body and your life in another way?

Maybe for you, neither of those things really apply, but you still don't feel great. You feel uncomfortable and anxious in your body when you wish you were confident and carefree. You can work toward that, too!

Too many of us feel embarrassed about our bodies. No matter who you are or how your body looks, it's never something to be ashamed of. Your body is the reason that you can do all the amazing things you do every day! Remember all the awesome ways your body takes care of you, and worry less about what other people think.

HONORING YOUR TRUE SELF

Maybe the possibility you care about is something completely different than what we've covered so far. Alternatively, maybe you've already done all the other stuff. You've already found a career that you love, you're financially stable and comfortable with your body... yet you still feel like something is missing. That's totally okay!

You can have so many parts of the equation right and still feel a little bit off. Usually, the thing that we're missing isn't something physical that needs to fall into place (although that could be it, too). It's something inside us that just needs a tweak in the right direction.

You might have developed a pessimistic attitude that makes you unsatisfied with yourself and everything you've achieved. Maybe mental health struggles have held you back from even considering the life you really want. You might not know what you want because you spent so long listening to what other people said you should want.

A lot of us have spent so long ignoring our inner self's voice. We listen to our inner critic instead, and that only holds us back more.

If you feel like everything in your life is great but you're still unhappy, maybe you need to do some digging into your true self. You might need to pull your feelings to the forefront, so you can get help with mental health concerns or reexamine the ways you're judging yourself. You might feel like you can't measure up to the standards other people are placing on you, but maybe those standards are what's wrong. Maybe you want to hold yourself to a completely different standard or abandon those rules entirely.

It's up to you to decide which parts of your life need to change, so you can love your life and honor your true self.

This is something you can definitely work toward as you read on!

WHAT A BADASS ISN'T

No matter who you are, you've got an inner badass in you somewhere. She's empowered, confident, and she knows exactly what she wants and how to get it. You're gonna find that part of you!

There's something you have to be wary of, though. In your quest for badassery, you might be tempted to compete with other people and push your way to the front of the pack. Standing up for yourself is amazing, but standing on top of others... not so much.

Being a true badass is the difference between being powerful and being forceful. You want to have the power to change your own life, help others, and be completely fulfilled by your choices. You don't want to push others down or force your way to the top.

The easiest way to make that difference is with confidence. You should be confident that your skills and prowess will speak for themselves. You don't need to speak over someone else because your power and your abilities shine on their own.

When you're a badass, you *know* your worth. That means there's no need to be pushy, aggressive, or competitive. If others don't see your value, you're better off without them.

A BADASS CHECK-IN

In this chapter, you learned that it's okay to have goals and dreams that are outside the norm. It's okay to start late from wherever you are. Your main goal is to become your truest self, and that involves looking long and hard at where you are and where you want to be. Maybe you can't achieve all your goals right this minute, or even this year, but you can still plan for the future.

You also hopefully got some ideas about who you want to become. You should be starting to ask yourself questions, like:

- What does being a badass mean to me?
- What's keeping me stuck, and how do I want to move away from that?

You don't need to have any clear-cut answers just yet. Your answer doesn't need to look like anyone else's, either. This journey is totally unique to you.

The most important thing to remember is that you're capable of changing your life for the better. You always have been! You just need to harness that power to move in the direction you want. That starts by figuring out what's holding you back.

2

WHAT'S HOLDING YOU BACK?

S urprisingly, it's not some big, all-powerful complex that's keeping you from getting unstuck. There isn't something terribly wrong with you.

You just keep telling yourself how bad you are in a bunch of little ways.

BAD VIBES

One of the biggest ways that you might hold yourself back is how you talk to and think about yourself.

A lot of this is completely subconscious, and it's more than just your inner critic. It's the story you tell about yourself and who you've decided that you are. You probably don't even notice yourself telling that story because it's so ingrained in you. It's become second nature.

What you *might* notice is that you ruminate on the bad stuff and do things that make you feel worse. So, if you do something wrong, you might be awake at night replaying what happened, feeling guilty, and imagining how much better things would have turned out if you had done it differently.

If you're having a bad day, you might do things that will keep you in a bad mood, like listening to sad music, turning down fun opportunities, and isolating yourself.

Now, don't get me wrong. There's nothing wrong with doing things like this once in a while. It can be freeing and healthy to let yourself feel sad or angry for the evening. It only becomes a problem when you're consistently keeping yourself down. There are so many ways that you might be doing this, but let's go over the most common ones.

Negative Self-Talk

Self-talk is, as you probably know, the way that you talk to yourself. It's the voice in your head as you go about your daily life, and it's the most obvious way that you could be sabotaging yourself.

When you look in the mirror, what do you say about yourself? Is it, "Ooh, I look good today!" or, "Oh no... is that what my nose looks like?" If it's the latter, you're practicing negative self-talk.

Negative self-talk is a way of speaking to yourself that makes you feel worse. The most obvious example is insulting your appearance, but you can also do this to yourself during conversations or throughout every aspect of your day. Some other examples of negative self-talk are:

- "That was a dumb thing to say."
- "Everyone must hate me now."
- "I'm such an embarrassment."
- "I'm so awkward."
- "I should be doing better than this."
- "Everyone must think I'm stupid/bad/selfish."

- *"Why is this so hard for me?"*

Do you frequently say things like this to yourself? If you do, don't feel bad. Negative self-talk is very common and almost encouraged. We're taught growing up to be humble and recognize our mistakes because no one likes a big ego. The thing is, a lot of us end up being humble to an extreme. We're quick to downplay our accomplishments and remind everyone around us (and ourselves) that we aren't that great.

It's nice to be humble, but having self-confidence is important, too! Start paying attention to how you speak to yourself.

Negative Narrative

Negative narrative is similar to negative self-talk, but it has one major difference. It's the story we're telling ourselves about who we are that *leads to* negative self-talk. For example, you might believe:

- "I'm a failure."
- "There's something wrong with me."
- "I always mess things up."

These harmful stories can result in negative self-talk and can keep us from making positive changes. If your life story is one where you can't ever succeed, you might decide there's no point in even trying.

What story are you telling yourself about who you are and how your life is? Do you think it's a positive one or a negative one?

It might be time to change the course of that story.

Limiting Beliefs

Limiting beliefs are what you think about yourself and people in your circumstances. Sometimes, internalized racism or misogyny plays a role here.

You might believe stereotypes about people like you, and that changes how you act and think about yourself. This can be in a general sense, like believing that all girls are bad at math. As a girl, this belief might hold you back from pursuing math and science as seriously as you pursue other career options. You might feel more anxious when you have a math test and be less sure of yourself—even when you know the answer. In fact, the slight difference in math performance between genders is probably caused by the stress of this stereotype (Ganley, 2018).

However, limiting beliefs can also be specific to you and your narrative. You might think that no one from your town will amount to anything, that single moms will have hard lives, or any number of other things about yourself and your circumstances.

This phenomenon is called *stereotype threat*. We tend to perform worse when we're fighting against a stereotype because of all the stress that it causes. After all, believing that everyone expects you to fail can make anything hard. When you hold limiting beliefs, you're doing this to yourself!

Think critically about how you're judging yourself based on what you've been through. What limiting beliefs do you hold about yourself and people like you? As we move forward, you'll start learning how to change these beliefs. For now, notice when you decide you can't do something and question why you think that.

Negative Programming

Do you feel like you're "too weird" or "too different" to be yourself around people? That's negative programming! Negative programming tells us that we can't make our own choices—instead, we have to do what everyone else is doing.

Sometimes, our brains are sneaky about it. You might say, "It's not worth it to try doing that; it'll never work" and never give that idea another thought. When we don't see other people doing what we want to, we might feel like it's impossible or never consider it in the first place.

You might feel like there's something wrong with you, and you have to hide it just to be accepted by others. Even if you don't feel that way, the pressure to conform can be overwhelming. We all have an intrinsic need to fit in, and that makes it hard to go against the grain. You don't want to be cast out from your friend groups for being different—even if your difference is what makes you feel alive.

Under these circumstances, forging your own path can feel totally impossible. It's something you need to overcome in small steps, but you'll eventually realize that the people you need in your life are the ones who accept your authentic self.

Tying It All Together

All of these factors can act together to influence your perceptions and decisions. When you have one of the above thoughts or feelings, try to decipher where it's coming from and why you feel that way. How does your negative self-talk tie in with your negative narrative and limiting beliefs?

What do you feel about where you came from and who your parents are? How do you feel about other people like you?

Keep in mind that your bad vibes are probably inherited. We tend to develop these negative thought patterns and beliefs when we see other people modeling them. You might have been told similar things as a child or grown up with poor self-esteem. No matter who you are or what you've been through, you deserve to heal.

YOU'RE LITERALLY BULLYING YOURSELF

You're probably doing at least one (and probably more) of the things from the list you just went through. You aren't the only one, and you shouldn't beat yourself up for it.

You *should* think about how drastically your negative programming, limiting beliefs, or negative self-talk have influenced your life. They might even be impacting your current thought processes and decisions.

Think about it this way: Your negative thought patterns tell you, in a million different ways, that *you are bad.* If you're walking around with a negative voice in your head, you're hearing that feedback constantly! What do you think that's doing to your self-esteem?

It's not helping—that's for sure!

Your inner critic makes you complacent by telling you that you deserve what you have, and you can't make a change.

"I Can't Change"

When you believe this lie about what you're capable of, you stop trying to make things better for yourself. You lose the spark that you had because you decide you aren't smart enough, strong enough, talented enough, or whatever it is that you think makes someone successful.

You'll equate success with being unlike yourself, which will make it even harder to succeed. You'll feel ashamed and hide who you are—all because you decided that you aren't good enough.

This is at the core of your negative beliefs, and it keeps you down. When you believe you can't change, you're in a vicious cycle. You feel unhappy and powerless to do anything about it. Any failed attempts to change will just reassure you that you're right: You really can't change.

But that's *not true!* Yes, change is hard, but it isn't impossible. When you have the right support system, you can do it. It might even be the hardest thing you ever do, but it will be worth it when you're finally living the life that you were meant for.

A sense of powerlessness is your greatest enemy when it comes to building a satisfying life. It keeps you trapped in situations that don't serve you because you don't think you can do any better.

When you pair this belief with the feeling that "this is what you deserve," things get even messier. You feel powerless to make a change, but you don't really want to make a change in the first place.

"This Is What I Deserve"

A lot of our negative self-perceptions center around the idea that we deserve it. We feel like it would be wrong to change our circumstances because that's where we belong.

If You Did Something Wrong

Maybe you did something that you still feel guilty about, and you haven't fully processed those feelings yet. Is that you? If so, you need to spend some time being compassionate with yourself. (Don't worry: You'll be learning this in later chapters; you don't have to do it alone!) We tend to focus on the bad things we've done and forget why we did them or what we've done since to fix them.

A great way to resolve guilt is to do something for the person you hurt—even if they never find out that it was you. You might give them a sincere apology if that hasn't happened yet or just do something nice for them. If this is someone that you've hurt deeply, understand that they might not want to have contact with you anymore. Sometimes, space is the best thing for both of you. Feeling guilty won't help the other person move on with their life. It'll only hurt you.

This is true—even if the person you hurt is still in your life. You might think that feeling guilty will make them feel better and understand how sorry you are. This is probably true right after you hurt them but not forever. They want to move on and acting sad will only draw out that process by reminding them of what happened.

You might only be able to earn their trust with time, but that doesn't mean you need to hold on to your guilt until then. If you had a negative self-concept to begin with, you've probably beaten yourself up plenty already.

Your guilt does not equal their healing, but your healing can help them heal.

Spend some time having compassion for the version of you that made this mistake. What were you feeling? The saying, "Hurt people hurt others" is truer than you might want to believe. It doesn't excuse your actions, but it can help you understand yourself. This work should be private and shouldn't be a way of writing off your behavior to the person who was hurt.

Write out how you were feeling, what was going through your mind at the time, and any recent life events that could have impacted you. Did you do the best you could at the time? Maybe not, but you did what you knew, and now, you know better.

This is an opportunity to grow—not an opportunity to keep yourself down.

If You Literally Did Nothing Wrong

Are you still feeling like you deserve to have a bad time—even though you did nothing wrong?

Let's think about that for a minute. You're thinking to yourself, *Yeah, I'm a decent human being, but I still deserve every bad thing that happens to me.*

Uh, what? How would you feel if you heard your best friend saying that?

Not only does it not make any sense, but it's also proof of a devastating self-concept. You believe that your existence is so awful that you don't have to do anything bad to deserve to suffer.

That's messed up!

Now, I'm not saying that to judge you. I'm saying it because I've been there, and it never made sense to me until a friend put it to me like that.

So how can we hold beliefs that don't make any sense?

Let me introduce you to the concept that will make it all make sense: *toxic shame.*

Toxic shame is a deep sense of shame about who you are as a person. You might feel broken, worthless, or that there's something seriously wrong with you. Whenever something bad happens, your first instinct will be that *you* must have done something wrong. You'll instantly feel ashamed of yourself whenever anyone is upset with you without thinking about if they're being reasonable.

This is different from normal guilt, which we feel when we do something wrong. It makes us feel bad when we hurt others, so we behave better in the future. Guilt has a purpose, but toxic shame doesn't.

Like debilitating self-beliefs, toxic shame doesn't exist in a vacuum. It's something that you adopt after repeated poor treatment when you're taught that you don't just do bad things or make mistakes sometimes—you *are* something bad (Golden, 2017).

Think about where you got these core beliefs from. When did

you first think that you weren't good enough? These feelings have to come from somewhere. They sometimes come up after we go through something traumatic, like a big rejection or hard time in our lives.

You might remember the first person who made you feel inferior. Who was it? Do you value their opinion now, and do you want it to run your life?

Of course not!

We tend to carry around other people's perceptions of us without thinking about if we value their opinion. We might have valued it once, but we don't have to value it now, especially when we see how much it's hurting us.

Negative self-perception doesn't help anyone except for the people who want you to fail. You don't want to be on their side; you want to prove them wrong!

The next chapter will help you figure out exactly where these feelings came from. It isn't that there's something wrong with you; it's that you were told (either implicitly or explicitly) that you aren't good enough.

Discovering the origin of your negative self-beliefs will help you see outside of them. You'll be able to see where the feeling is coming from, so it doesn't have the same power over you. It won't be able to make you miserable anymore.

You Matter

The key takeaway from everything you've learned so far is that you make a difference in the outcome of your life. Right now, you're making a difference in a negative way. You're constantly beating yourself up, telling yourself you aren't good enough, and letting shame hold you back.

What you've been through caused you to hold on to these negative beliefs and feelings, but now, you're weaponizing them against yourself.

Imagine that you're being constantly followed by someone who makes negative comments about your choices, how you look, and how you spend your time. This frenemy follows you everywhere. They fall asleep beside you, and when you wake up, they're already complaining.

That's what you're doing to yourself!

It's no wonder that you feel exhausted and unable to change. You've created an environment of toxicity, shame, and self-hatred. No one can thrive like that, and that's why you're failing: You literally set yourself up for it.

If you can make yourself feel totally miserable and incompetent, can't the opposite be true?

If your inner voice can be absolute hell to be around and make your life 90% harder than it has to be, it can also make things easier for you. You just have to change the way you're using it, and that starts with understanding where it came from.

A BADASS CHECK-IN

You just learned about a bunch of things that are keeping you from becoming your truest, most badass self. They're how you keep yourself from succeeding. Your negative attitude and poor self-esteem don't just make you feel awful; they also can keep you from making the positive changes that are necessary to live the life you want!

When you let these negative feelings reign, you're letting your bad past experiences control you. It's impossible to embrace your inner badass when you're unconsciously reminding yourself of all the reasons it can't work out.

That's why it's so important to notice these negative thoughts and beliefs, so you can stop them in their tracks. Ditching these negative self-perceptions is crucial to developing the confidence of your inner badass! It'll be easier to do that when you know where you got these feelings from, so that's what we'll do next.

Side Note: This would be a great time to try my workbook! It has tons of exercises to help you figure out what you want and become your most badass self. It's the perfect companion to this book and will help you to process everything you've been learning here. Grab your copy for free! You can find the link at the end of the conclusion.

The exercises in the workbook will help you delve more deeply into the topics we cover and get the most out of all the work you're doing to improve your life. I recommend starting it now before we get too far along in the process!

3

WHERE THE JUNK COMES FROM

You've absorbed a lot of information about your bad habits and how much they're holding you back. Now, it's time to figure out exactly where they're coming from, so you can have more compassion for yourself and finally break the cycle!

I DON'T WANT TO SAY IT'S YOUR CHILDHOOD, BUT…

Yeah, it's your childhood (at least partly).

First off, if you aren't ready to dig deep into what you've been through and how it forged your current habits, that's okay! Feel free to skip this section. The whole point of learning about your childhood is to notice your feelings and be kinder to yourself. If you don't feel ready to tackle this topic just yet, then come back to it another time.

As much as we hate to admit it, the way we're brought up plays a huge part in our adult thoughts and behaviors. As children, we learn what normal behavior is and mimic the adults we spend time with.

A child's world is tiny. It might be as small as your parents and your immediate family, and it could stay like that until first grade. That means that you picked up thought patterns and behaviors at a young and impressionable age, with nothing else to compare them to. You might have adopted other behaviors throughout your childhood as you went to school and made friends, but that's where it all started.

Sometimes, those early skills are helpful. You parents might have taught you how to explore safely, share, and get along with others. There might have been some less helpful teachings in there, too.

You might pride yourself on being nothing like your family. If you grew up with hurtful family members, you might have vowed to never be like them.

The thing is, your childhood still impacts who you are as an adult—*even if you're nothing like your family.* If you're trying really hard not to be like someone else, you still aren't being fully yourself. You're just making a persona that's unlike your family. Your true self probably has some traits from your parents and some that you picked up from other people.

This can be hard to grapple with. You might have built your whole personality around being a leader because you watched meek family members get pushed around. Maybe you're afraid to be vulnerable because you've learned that vulnerability only gets you hurt, so you started isolating yourself.

To overcome the bad habits you learned growing up, you have to notice what they are and where you picked them up. A lot of them are learned in childhood because we tend to pick up a lot of our core beliefs during that time. However, your family isn't the only influence on your beliefs.

Your self-perception can be influenced by anyone else you knew growing up and by events in your adult life. So, if the whole, "Your childhood made you like this" thing doesn't sit right with you, the last section in this chapter is for you.

Childhood and the Brain

Your childhood doesn't just influence how you feel about yourself; it literally changes your brain. As we're growing up, our brains are forming new connections and figuring out how the world works. If the way you grew up didn't reflect the real world, you ended up navigating adulthood with a brain that doesn't quite get it.

Growing up in a less-than-ideal environment—which, let's face it, everyone does—changes how your brain processes information (Dye, 2018). Childhood trauma can lead to mental, physical, and emotional symptoms in your adult life. These symptoms can include anything from fatigue and high stress to depression and post-traumatic stress disorder (PTSD) (Majer et al., 2010).

Your brain formed connections around a world that doesn't exist anymore: the tiny world you grew up in. You might have adapted to mistreatment or lived in constant fear. Now, you're trying to navigate the real world in the same way. It can be hard to survive in that environment, let alone thrive.

You don't have to go through something traumatic to have this problem, though. Most people pick up at least a couple unhelpful coping mechanisms before they grow up. Even overprotective parents can make things rough in your adult life. Kids are perceptive, and they notice how their caretakers respond to things. They intuitively pick up on their habits and behaviors. If your caretakers respond to new things with fear and apprehension, you'll grow up responding to them the same way. Some of these patterns can be changed over time, but others stick around.

Defining Childhood Moments

Is there a point in your life with a distinct before and after—

something that changed how you see yourself and the world? That's a defining moment.

These moments are where we developed certain patterns, fears, or beliefs. It could be the death of a loved one, divorcing parents, or a huge family fight. Different people are affected by different things, so don't judge yourself for whatever your defining moments might be.

Remember: You don't just have negative defining moments. For the purpose of this book, we're focusing on where you may have picked up negative beliefs and feelings about yourself. To make a list that fully reflects your experience, don't forget to include the positive ones, too.

Some common ones are:

- Falling out with a family member
- Ongoing family conflict
- Finding a passion
- Yourself or a loved one getting sick
- Bullying
- Changing schools
- Losing or gaining a friend
- Family drama
- Going through mental illness (yourself or someone close to you)

Make a list of moments that had a big influence on you growing up. What were they? What were you like before and after they happened?

As you sort through your memories, you're bound to experience a roller coaster of emotions. You might feel angry or sad about what happened to you or feel guilty for being affected by something that seems small. Remember: There's no shame in being affected by your memories. You are allowed to feel the way you feel. It doesn't make you less.

In fact, processing these feelings will help you move forward because your defining moments probably caused a lot of your negative thought patterns.

It might seem strange that kids can get a negative self-image from bad things that happen to them—even if they did nothing wrong. Unfortunately, that's exactly what happens.

Kids can't believe that their caregivers are bad at taking care of them and for good reason. Children can't handle worrying about whether they're safe on top of the whole ordeal of growing up. So, if kids experience hardship or bad treatment, they assume they're the problem. It couldn't possibly be their parents—the ones who know everything, feed them, and are their only way of surviving in the world, right?

That's why so many adults think there's something wrong with them. They learned this faulty way of thinking because they needed it to survive. They had to believe they were the problem to feel safe and protected.

This thought process doesn't serve anyone in adulthood, but it can be so hard to shake. You might even assume it's just part of your personality.

Going forward, remember where your negative self-perception and limiting beliefs came from. You developed them as a way to survive your childhood, but they aren't helping you anymore.

Repeat after me: There is nothing wrong with you!

You can unlearn these behaviors to have a more satisfying, joyful life.

PTSD and C-PTSD

An event in your life might have been more than a defining moment. It didn't just make you different; it scarred you. You might have nightmares (and flashbacks), anxiety, trouble sleeping, or intrusive thoughts. If that's you, you might have PTSD.

A lot of people think it's something that doesn't happen to people like them. PTSD is something that people get when they're on a literal battlefield or get in a bad accident, right?

Well, not exactly. Even if you didn't go through something terrifying and unusual, you could still have PTSD. It stems from an event that was traumatic *to you*. That will depend on who you are, what you were used to, and what you were going through at the time. Natural disasters, abuse, threats, or the loss of a loved one can all be traumatic events. Plus, you don't have to go through something like this yourself to be traumatized (Hasan, 2018). Seeing someone you love get threatened or be abused can be traumatizing for them and for you.

Complex post-traumatic stress disorder (C-PTSD) is a different type of PTSD. It happens when you have prolonged exposure to something traumatic. So, instead of dealing with one major life event, you dealt with an ongoing, traumatizing situation. C-PTSD can occur if you went through abuse, neglect, abandonment, or another kind of ongoing trauma.

You're more likely to suffer from C-PTSD if you experienced trauma at an early age, had no way of escape, or were hurt by someone close to you (Mind, 2021). It causes many of the same symptoms as PTSD, with some additional ones, like:

- Feeling empty
- Difficulty handling your emotions
- Being distrusting or fearful
- Avoiding relationships or struggling with them
- Experiencing body pains, like headaches and stomachaches
- Feeling disconnected from yourself and others (dissociation)

If something you went through had a strong impact on your life, you're not alone. Harsh experiences in childhood *and* adulthood can leave you with unresolved trauma that influences every aspect of your life. If you're dealing with the symptoms of PTSD or C-PTSD, reach out to your doctor or a licensed therapist to help you find the support you deserve.

WHERE ELSE CAN IT COME FROM?

Maybe your childhood was pretty laid back, and you can't think of anything that had a dramatic impact on you. There might be a few little things, but nothing that would explain how you feel.

Not to worry: This section is for you.

Adult Relationships Can Mess You Up, Too

If you thought that only your childhood could mess you up, well... sorry. It's pretty common to have adult relationships that change your outlook on life. They can leave you with a bitter taste in your mouth or a completely different view of yourself—all depending on the circumstances.

Late Bloomers

One of the most common reasons to be thrown off by an adult relationship is being a late bloomer. If you had overprotective parents or were busy in high school, you might not have had all the stereotypical teenage experiences.

Even though you're probably familiar with the term, being a "late bloomer" doesn't make you late at all. It's common to have a lot of the firsts we associate with teenagers in our 20s or 30s. There's nothing shameful about that; you're actually better off for it.

It means that you waited to have your first relationship until your brain was more fully developed, which saved you a lot of teenage heartache. The thing is, your first relationships will have a big impact on you as an adult, as well.

Your brain might be more developed and better at handling emotions, but it's still your first time having that experience. You probably aren't going to get it right on the first try, and that first breakup is always a doozy.

Even though you're avoiding the developing brain issue, there's something else at play that makes this hard. Since you're doing your firsts later than your friends (or later than they claim they did), you might feel more pressure to get it right and be more freaked out by a breakup. You can feel like you have to settle down because you don't have much time to waste.

This can cause unnecessary stress on you and your partner. You might mess up good relationships because you feel pressured to find the "perfect person." On the other hand, you might stick with someone you know is wrong for you because you're scared that you won't find anyone else.

If it makes you feel any better, most of that is BS. You have more time than you think to figure everything out. There are tons of people in the world that you could meet and create a loving relationship with. You just have to decide if the one in front of you is the one you want to make it work with. If not, there are so many other people out there. But, if this is what you both want, you can make it work long term with a whole lot of love, communication, and commitment. There is no countdown going on behind the scenes. You don't have to be married by 30 to be a "real woman" like your mother or grandmother might think. Do things on your own terms and in your own way.

Casual Sex

First of all, if you're out there having a good time and have no qualms with your situation, this isn't about you. Keep doing your thing, girl!

But, if you had (or are having) casual sex and it leaves you feeling kind of weird, here's why.

A lot of people tend to lean into casual sex to replace something else in their life, especially during a period of transition. It's very common among people fresh out of a relationship, who are moving soon, or who don't want to settle down for another reason. It's a way of finding human connection and closeness without putting in as much time and effort.

It becomes a problem when you're filling a void with sex that you want to replace with something else. You might look back on a time like this in your life and see that you were simply lonely and looking for closeness.

Let's get back to that "time and effort" problem. When you're already feeling down, meeting up with other people who don't want to spend much time or effort on you can leave you feeling worse. This is especially true when it comes to sex, which can be a super vulnerable experience.

It can leave you with an implicit feeling that you aren't worth someone else's time and energy or that your body is your most valuable asset. So, if you had a period like this in your life that felt wrong to you, it might have left you with negative beliefs like this.

Messy Breakups

Adult breakups can be just as devastating as teenage ones, especially if you didn't see them coming or had big future plans.

There are a few different reasons that a breakup might have hit you hard. You might have felt like your partner was "the one" and struggle to grapple with life without them. Maybe it was a long time coming, and it was hard to admit that things weren't working out. If you were in an abusive relationship and had to find a way out, that can be extremely traumatic.

Any of these experiences could be a source of negative self-image. After bad breakups or hurtful relationship experiences, we tend to focus on what we did wrong and how we could've been better partners. You might feel guilty or angry about what was said and how things turned out, which can lead to rumination.

You can be left with an uneasy feeling that you're a worse person than you thought or that you didn't deserve your partner. You might question your relationship skills and start avoiding them altogether.

The same feelings can arise from friend breakups. It's not just our romantic partners that influence our sense of self. If you had a close friendship that ended poorly, that can leave you with a battered self-image, too.

Loneliness

You might start to feel like other people are the enemy. It can seem like other people are always leaving you hurt and changed. Maybe you're better off alone, right?

The thing is, being lonely also takes a toll on your sense of self over time.

Loneliness is a symptom of disconnect. It makes you want to form connections because in caveman times, we were safer in groups. Unfortunately, this is still true today in a lot of ways, especially for women.

Prolonged loneliness can impact your ability to build new relationships because it makes you question yourself and your worth. You might feel incapable of making new friends, like you're a burden to others, or that you'll never meet anyone you can connect with.

So many of our negative beliefs can be amplified or formed from periods of loneliness.

THE CHICKEN OR THE EGG?

So far, we've talked about how our early experiences can influence who we are and how we feel about ourselves, but that isn't the only factor at play.

Bad childhood experiences commonly lead to negative self-image, but poor self-esteem can lead to worse life experiences, too. People with lower self-esteem are more likely to isolate themselves, settle for poorer social connections, and accept loneliness instead of making friends (Kansky, 2018). For those reasons, it can be hard to tell if poor self-esteem is causing the less satisfying relationships, or vice versa.

Often, it's a combination of both. You might have had bad experiences that compromised your self-esteem in childhood and led to more isolation as an adult. Take a moment to think about what had a bigger influence on you.

THE BADASS CHECK-IN

Our childhood and early adult experiences change our perceptions of ourselves—for better or for worse. They can leave us with lingering feelings of unworthiness or anxiety that follow us until we can resolve them. Negative experiences can make us feel unsafe around other people and make us prone to isolation. Unfortunately, that comes with its own baggage.

Our early experiences with relationships and loneliness change what we expect from the future. They can set us up to have positive, fulfilling adult relationships... or not. These defining moments can make you want to build walls and protect yourself from the world, which can make things even more complicated.

Being aware of your unique upbringing and adult experiences will help you to notice where your negative beliefs are coming from, so you can keep them from taking control of your life.

After all, the key to being a badass isn't to avoid these feelings or experiences altogether. It's to work through them and come out the other side even stronger and more confident. It's incredibly empowering to see where these feelings are coming from, honor their place in your past, and decide that they aren't helping you anymore.

You can choose to reject the parts of your past that aren't worth bringing into your future. You deserve to feel good about yourself!

4

THE BRAIN-BODY CONNECTION

There's a deeper connection between your body and your brain, and it's probably why you feel awful. See, all those negative childhood experiences and bad feelings you've been holding on to can impact your body.

We tend to think of our bodies and minds as separate things. Our thoughts don't impact our body, and our body doesn't really impact our thoughts. Right?

Wrong!

Scientists are just starting to figure out how much our brains and bodies are connected. It turns out that even the bacteria in your gut can be connected with your mental health. Recent research from Malan-Miller et al. (2018) suggests that gut microbiome is related to anxiety and trauma disorders. This proves that mental health isn't just something that happens in your mind. It's deeply connected to your body and experience of the world (Lucas, 2018).

So what does this mean for you? It means that you can't heal your brain without healing your body, too; it's a package deal.

On one hand, this means that improving your mental health

can improve your physical health. As you heal emotionally and mentally, physical healing will come with it. But it also means that full healing has to involve both your body and your mind.

WHY YOU FEEL LIKE CRAP

Unfortunately, the brain-body connection also means that your mental health can mess up your physical health. Have you ever heard the saying, "The body keeps the score?" Unfortunately, it's accurate.

It means that feeling stuck mentally can leave you physically stuck, too. You might have lost your hold on some positive habits, like healthy eating or being active. Feeling guilty about being inactive and eating junk food makes you feel worse, and all of a sudden, you're in a shame spiral.

This saying also explains a lot of the physical symptoms that we feel when we're stuck. You might have any of the following (Firth et al., 2019):

- Bloating
- Fatigue
- Trouble sleeping (either too much or not enough)
- Unexplained body/joint pain
- Headaches
- Skin changes (breakouts, rashes, or texture changes)

These physical symptoms show just how much your mind impacts your body. All that negative energy has to go somewhere. You might not think that beating yourself up is a problem, but it's doing real damage to your body.

It might seem like all of these physical problems are coming out of nowhere, but they make sense when you think about them. When you feel stuck, you're more likely to be anxious, stressed, or depressed (or a triple threat with all of them). Anxiety and stress make you more tense, which can lead to more headaches and body aches. You might also slouch if you're feeling low, which can increase body pain. All three of these can make it hard to sleep, which can leave you with even more aches, poor skin, fatigue, and digestion problems.

If you're dealing with any kind of mental illness, that can make it harder to access health care, too. Doctors are more likely to write off your symptoms as a result of your mental illness instead of treating them. This leaves so many women suffering from multiple health issues without treatment for any of them.

It totally sucks, but it's important to be aware of things like this. Your doctor probably knows a lot more about health than you, but they don't know your body the way you do. If you ever see a doctor who brushes you off or refuses to help you, go see someone else!

Any symptoms that you're dealing with, physically or mentally, are not your fault.

Read that again: They're not your fault! You didn't do anything wrong to deserve what's happening to you, but here's the thing. Your symptoms *are* your responsibility.

As much as we all want to be carried away by some charming lover into perfect health and happiness, we have to admit to ourselves that it doesn't work that way. Even the most perfect person for you can't totally heal you.

That includes doctors, therapists, and anyone else in your life. Other people can help you on your journey, but you have to put in the work to heal.

Not only that but getting better so you can enjoy your life is honestly the biggest responsibility you have. No matter what happens to you, the only thing guaranteed to you is your life at this very moment. If you're spending that time being totally miserable... sure, you can blame a lot of people for all the bad things that have happened. But you're the only one who can put in the work to make it different. Not to get super deep, but isn't enjoying your life the one real point of being here?

To start taking steps in the right direction, you have to accept that being your own bully is the opposite of helpful.

Let that motivate you to be kinder to your body and your mind.

So what do you do about those physical symptoms that are keeping you stuck? Well, a lot of it is about adjusting your mindset, which we'll be focusing on in Chapter 6. But, for now, you'll want to focus on just being kind to yourself and your body.

You'll be surprised by how much some simple changes can make you feel better. For some of you, it might just be an act of self-love that helps you feel more positive. For others, it could reduce or totally resolve your symptoms. Regardless, it's worth a shot!

HOW TO FEEL BETTER

Now, if you're about to flip away because you think I'm about to push a new diet on you or tell you to get up at 5 a.m. and go to the gym, hold on: Let me explain.

Sure, some people might feel better after going to the gym or drinking green juice, but that might not be for you—not now and maybe not ever. So, instead of working out and eating salad, I'm challenging you to do what feels good to your body.

Do what makes you excited to get up, and don't do things that make you feel crappy afterward. This will probably take some experimentation to get right, but it'll be worth it.

Right now, you might be eating tons of junk food, totally restricting yourself, or just have an average relationship with food. Wherever you are, this advice will help you feel better. It counts for both exercise and healthy eating, too. Sure, it's great if you eat lots of veggies and have a regular workout routine, but your top priority is your own satisfaction.

You've been stuck in a rut. When you're in that headspace, it's easy to nosedive into diet culture or a strict workout routine that makes you miserable. It can be another way of punishing yourself when you're unhappy with your circumstances. Don't worry about all of that.

Don't Try to Change Your Body

We tend to go into dietary and lifestyle changes to change our body. You might want to look better in that swimsuit or feel more attractive. As women, we base so much of our value on our appearance.

For this change to work, you have to fight against the idea that positive change will provide instant physical results. Healing won't make you lose 10 pounds, and that's a *good thing*. This section is about healing your relationship with food and exercise without worrying what your body looks like.

You aren't healing for other people; you're healing for yourself. That's what your eating and movement should be like, too.

Loving Food

If you feel amazing after eating a bowl of chips, cool! If you want to die every time you taste spinach (girl, same), then don't eat it. It's okay if you eat more junk than usual. It's okay if you gain a few pounds. *It's okay.*

Eat whatever you want and pay attention to how it makes your body feel.

What will probably happen is that when you stop denying yourself all the "fun foods" that you really love, like chips or chocolate, they'll eventually stop being so magical. You might notice that you always get an upset stomach when you eat sweets, or you feel bloated when you aren't drinking enough water. Maybe you can eat six chocolates and feel amazing, but seven will leave you feeling nauseated.

You'll eventually find the balance that works for you—one that includes all sorts of food that you love and that make you feel good, including chips, chocolate, candy, *and* veggies plus protein. Hopefully, all the foods you eat will make you happy.

Eventually, it won't feel like your chips or candy are "bad," and your veggies are "good." They're all just different foods that benefit you in different ways, and you can love them for that.

Movement That Doesn't Make You Miserable

You'll want to have the same approach when it comes to movement. I'm hesitant to even call it "exercise" because it shouldn't feel like a fitness thing. It should be a for-fun thing with fitness as an extra bonus.

Do you love dancing, swimming, or yoga? Maybe you like to go on hikes or walks. Which activities do you genuinely love? If it's hard to think of something, that's totally fine. Is there something you've always wanted to try? Now's your chance to try it!

If all you want to do is some light morning stretches, you do you. I'm not here to tell you that you *need* to do some heart-pumping exercise or even be active at all. I'm not your doctor. If the concept of exercise in any capacity makes you grumpy, I'm obviously not going to force you. I mean, let's be honest: I couldn't if I wanted to.

I will challenge you to just *try something*. Maybe you want to try to touch your toes every morning until you can do it (I certainly can't) or go for a quick walk around the block after work.

Try to find one thing you can do that gets your body moving and makes you feel good. The unfortunate truth is that our bodies were designed to be active, and we usually feel better when we're getting a bit more activity in our day. Just try it out and see if it works for you.

Sleep Hygiene

Having trouble sleeping, a weird sleep schedule, or some combination of the two?

Sleep hygiene is the process of making good habits around sleep, and it's an easy way to solve common sleep problems. It's a good thing to address while you're figuring out what feels best to your body in terms of food and exercise.

Most sleep problems have to do with your bed and what you do in it. If you're the kind of person who likes to lay in bed watching TV all weekend, you're doing it wrong!

In general, your bed should only be for sleep and sex. Don't make a habit of watching TV or movies in bed and try to make it a phone-free zone. Using your phone is a stimulating activity that can make it harder to sleep, whether you've got a blue light filter or not (Cárthaigh et al., 2020). It's true that blue light is partially responsible for sleep disturbances, but it isn't the only factor. Using your phone is also an addictive activity. You've literally got the world at your fingertips, which makes it hard to put the phone down and get to sleep.

Now, I know that's a hard pill to swallow, so if using your phone is part of your nightly ritual and doesn't impact your sleep, go ahead and use it. Just make sure that you have a bedtime routine, so your body knows when it's time for sleep.

A good bedtime routine doesn't have to start at the same time, although that can be comforting for some people. If you already brush your teeth or take off your makeup before bed, you're on the right track. Little habits like this tell your body that it's time for bed, and you can combine them to make a more satisfying routine.

For example, you might start by changing into your pajamas and then brushing your teeth and taking your makeup off. At that point, you might climb into bed and read for a bit, watch a relaxing video, or just pass out. Maintaining a simple pattern like that can make a world of difference.

If you do want to change your sleep schedule, make incremental changes instead of doing it all at once. Move your sleep and wake-up times backward or forward by no more than an hour or two every night (Suni, 2020). In general, it's best to wake up at the same time every day—even on weekends. Take a nap when you're tired instead of sleeping in on the weekend.

Overall, these sleep hygiene tips should help you to make a few small but impactful adjustments. Try them out if you've been having trouble sleeping or want to establish a better routine.

A BADASS CHECK-IN

Throughout this chapter, you've learned to notice what feels good in your body. It might feel weird at first, especially if you're used to being strict with yourself.

I want to help you realize that being kind to yourself makes your life better and easier. You aren't successful because you're hard on yourself. In fact, being hard on yourself holds you back. Being a badass isn't about controlling every aspect of your life to make it perfect. It's about finding a way of life that suits you, no matter how unconventional, and honoring it! As you learn to honor your body—including your hunger, aches, and everything else that comes with it—you're learning your inherent worth. Guess what? A crucial part of being a badass is knowing your worth and not settling for less!

Plus, when you're well rested, being active in ways you like, and eating food that makes you feel good, you'll be more productive. Plus, you'll be less miserable, which is more important.

5

ATTACHMENTS (AND LACK THEREOF)

There are probably things you do every day that make it harder to get better. Your daily habits and even your closest friends could be keeping you stuck. Without realizing it, you're setting the standard for what you'll put up with in your life... and you're setting it *way* too low. This impacts your happiness, self-esteem, and even your time. You might spread yourself too thin because you can't say no to anyone.

Your attachment style determines how much you'll put up with from other people. It's one step deeper than your negative beliefs, thoughts, or programming. It's the way that you naturally feel around others. Almost everyone has a quirk when it comes to attachment, and these quirks aren't necessarily a problem. They become harmful when you'd rather have mean friends than spend some time alone or totally isolated instead of having a subpar friend. There's got to be some balance in there.

Over time, these problems snowball into mountains. They make us cling to others or drive them away until we end up in a bad situation. Starting to heal can feel pointless when you're looking up at Everest. If that's where you're at, you've got to stop building up the mountain!

These are the patterns and people in your life that are keeping you stuck, and you need to learn how to stop them.

ARE THEY BRINGING YOU DOWN?

Do you have any friends that you don't actually like to hang out with?

Some people in your life are only there because you feel an obligation to keep them there. If you:

- dread hanging out with them,
- only spend time with them out of obligation,
- feel like they don't care about understanding you,
- are getting put down or made fun of—even as a joke,
- know they're a bad influence on you (they encourage you to do stuff you regret),
- bad-mouth them to your other friends, or
- feel worse about yourself after seeing them for any reason…

… then you don't have to hang out with them! This might be controversial, but I believe that everyone deserves friends who like them and that they like back.

Obligatory Friendships

Hanging out with someone out of obligation doesn't feel good to them, and it doesn't feel good to you, either! When you only spend time with someone because you have to, you act differently. People notice that!

It's not the charitable call that you think it is, and here's why: *Friendships are just a different kind of dating.*

You might not be looking for love and attraction, but you are looking for compatibility in a different sense, right? You want friends that you can be yourself around with the same sense of humor. You want to hang out with people who love the weird stuff you love and want to talk about it as much as you do.

When you're hanging out with someone out of obligation, you're doing the friendship equivalent of stringing them along. You're making them feel like there's a real chance at closeness while holding them at arm's length.

It's kind of crappy.

Even if they love hanging out with you, they'll never get the friendship they crave from you. You're better off telling them that you're unavailable, so they'll start finding other friends who genuinely want to spend time with them.

This is better for them because they won't be hanging out with someone who low-key doesn't want to be there, but it's also way better for you. You won't be obligated to hang out, and you'll know that you did the right thing by encouraging them to find other friends.

Give yourself the freedom to say that you're busy this week, and the next... and maybe the one after that.

Bad Influences

When you think of friends that are bad influences, you might think of people that you drink or smoke with or people that encourage you to mess up your diet. All of these might be bad influences, but there are some you're probably forgetting.

If a friend is always talking about losing weight and you always end up crash dieting after you see them, they're a bad influence! If someone has terrible self-esteem and you end up one-upping each other about how crappy you feel, they're a bad influence! If they're negative about everything and it brings you down, you guessed it— bad influence!

The problem is that these are the toughest types of friends to let go of. They're the people that you might really like to hang out with, but you know they aren't good for you in the long run. You might have a lot in common and bond over your self-sabotaging behaviors. They make you feel like you're not alone.

Bad influence friends are more than just people you bond over mistakes with or call when you want to go drinking. They're the ones that make you do things you end up regretting over and over.

Now, they might not be doing it on purpose, which can make the whole situation more confusing. They might just be using their own flawed coping mechanisms and be happy to have you along for the ride. But, if you always end up feeling awful after you hang out, it doesn't matter!

If you know your "bad influence" friend is a good person who is just a little mixed up themselves, ask them to do something different from your usual activity. If you always go drinking or talk about how awful you both feel, invite them over for a game night instead. Finding something else to bond over will make your friendship more dynamic and keep you from being stuck in their bad vibes. You've got your own to worry about!

Besides, your friend might not even notice the negative impact they're having on other people. If their negativity makes you cancel your plans, telling them that might be the wake-up call they need. It might help them recognize just how pessimistic they're being and start reigning it in for their own mental health.

People-Pleasing

Are you a notorious people-pleaser?

That can be the root of so many unsatisfying connections. You might stick with friends you don't really like because you don't want to let them down or make them feel bad.

People-pleasing tends to stem from a feeling of inadequacy. Deep down, you might feel like you aren't worthy of your friends if you aren't doing everything in your power to make things great for them.

You might have grown up in a family of people-pleasers or been taught by your parents that you should cater to other people. Maybe you just don't know any different.

If you're like me, you might be eager to please your friends but feel disheartened when they aren't going above and beyond for you, too. You might think to yourself, *I'm being such a good friend to Sarah by always letting her pick where we eat. She should do more for me.*

Get this: People-pleasing doesn't make you a better friend.

Constantly giving up what you want to please someone else is just a recipe for resentment. Over time, you'll get more and more frustrated that the other person isn't doing "as much" as you are.

Basically, your friend is screwed no matter what. Either they catch on and start frantically trying to guess what you want (which is almost impossible when you never say what that is) or they end up with a really resentful friend and don't understand why.

Plus, you might not even be giving them what they want. What you want isn't necessarily what your friend wants. Letting your friend pick where you eat might just make her uncomfortable, especially if she doesn't know a lot of restaurants.

For that reason, giving your friend the option that you want can keep you *both* from having what you want. Your friend is stuck with the thing you generously gave away when they actually wanted something else.

Of course, if your friend just tells you how they feel or what they want, you won't get into such a confusing situation. It's at its worst when two people-pleasers get together. That means both of you will try to give the other person what *you* wanted and be too shy to speak up about what you wanted.

It's hard to stop people-pleasing, but it's totally possible. You have to start paying attention to your desires—not just someone else's. Once you're aware of how you really feel in a situation, it gets easier to express that to someone else.

How Is This Related to Attachment, Anyway?

The answer is that *all* of these behaviors can be explained or exacerbated by an anxious attachment style. Anxiously attached people are often afraid to be alone. They might worry that their friends will leave them if they don't people-please, and they'll stay with bad friends because they would rather do that than be alone. You might be worried about what other people are thinking and feel responsible for their emotions. (Hint: You're not!)

Anxious attachment style often comes from inconsistent parenting (The Attachment Project, 2020). When you were growing up, your caregivers might have only responded to you sometimes or given affection in certain conditions. That kind of environment primes you to feel unsure. You don't know if you can rely on the people around you because sometimes, they meet your needs, but other times, they don't.

On the other hand, your parents might have sought connection with you to make *them* happy—not to make *you* happy. They might have wanted to be seen as perfect parents, so they treated you in ways that would make them look best but didn't necessarily do what was best for you. Alternatively, they simply wanted to feel love and connection and sought it from their child. If you had parents like this, you might have grown up feeling that your parents were overprotective or constantly looking over your shoulder.

Keep in mind that your parents aren't necessarily bad people for doing this. They're simply repeating the same patterns that they learned.

This can make you hyper-focused on other people. You might have learned that people-pleasing will help you get your needs met or stay safe as a child, so you've brought that behavior with you into adulthood.

You don't have to go through any trauma to have an anxious attachment style, either. Nonideal parenting styles are common, and you can end up anxiously attached just because your mom was busy with work and wasn't always around. If you noticed that agreeing with other people kept you from getting into fights with your siblings, that could have contributed. It's not just the big stuff that changes your attachment; it's the little things that build up.

Having an anxious attachment style doesn't mean you have a mental health disorder, and it might not be a cause for concern. However, this style of attachment can make your relationships more difficult. Knowing how you connect with other people will help you better understand your reactions and emotions.

Ideally, you want to have a secure attachment where you feel comfortable and safe being yourself with your friends and loved ones. As you open up about what you want, this might happen naturally. If it doesn't, that's fine. Just pay attention to how it goes for you.

How to Properly Execute a Friend Breakup

If you want to get away from a friendship that isn't serving you anymore, you basically have three options:

- Come clean: Tell them that you aren't feeling the friendship, and you want to help introduce them to other people. This is the most honest thing to do but also the hardest and most confrontational. Use it at your own risk.

- Ghost 'em: Literally just stop replying to them. This is ethically the worst option but also the easiest.
- The long con: Start spacing out your meetups and replying to messages slower. Tell them you're really busy and gradually hang out less and less until you stop altogether. This mimics what happens when people fall out of touch, so it's probably the nicest and least confrontational. It's also the most work, though.

These are all useful in certain situations. For example, if the "friend" is possibly dangerous or is making your life extremely difficult, you might be better off just ghosting them. It all depends on the person in question, so use your best judgment to choose the right method for you.

CHOOSING LONELINESS

Maybe you can't relate to the whole concept of being afraid to be alone. You might feel safest and happiest when you're alone because you don't have to worry about other people. You're good at taking care of yourself and could happily spend week after week alone in your apartment.

Is that you? If that's the case, you probably don't have the same issues with unsatisfying friends that the anxiously attached person does. It might be really hard to get close to you because you're content being by yourself. You might even be freaked out when people try to get to know you too fast. You, my friend, probably have an avoidant attachment style.

Patterns of Isolation and Avoidant Attachment

If you have an avoidant attachment style, you already know that you'll be more likely to isolate yourself. This tendency usually comes from a feeling that other people aren't safe and can't contribute anything to your life. And, you guessed it—it starts in childhood.

Dismissive vs. Fearful Avoidant

Depending on your upbringing and early experiences, you'll probably be either a dismissive avoidant or fearful avoidant type, and there's a big difference between them.

Dismissive avoidant types are the typical avoidant type. As a rule, they want to avoid closeness with other people and feel threatened by intimacy. If you're a dismissive avoidant, you're highly independent and feel brought down by connections to others. You don't like to rely on others or have them relying on you.

You're also likely to suppress your feelings because you believe it makes things easier. You might lash out to push people away when you feel threatened, which helps you maintain the space you crave.

This style is created when caregivers usually don't meet your needs. Babies with these kinds of parents don't tend to react emotionally when their caregivers leave and aren't clingy when they get back (Raimondi, 2019). They've learned not to expect comfort from others and instead self-soothe or feel unbothered by being alone.

People with this attachment style might have experienced neglect as a child (physical, emotional, or otherwise), or they might have had busy parents and learned to handle things by themselves.

Once again, having this attachment style doesn't mean there's something wrong with you. If you're happy where you are, there's nothing wrong with that! But you might be starting to see why attachment styles can cause conflict with other people. If you have a friend with an anxious attachment style, they can be confused by your isolating tendencies and feel rejected. Their desire for closeness will make you uncomfortable, and things can spiral from there. Being aware of your style and how it relates to other people can make you more understanding when these conflicts come up. It'll help you explain that your need for space doesn't mean you don't love them.

If you relate to both the anxious and dismissive styles, you're probably a fearful avoidant, also known as a disorganized type. This style is characterized by a mix of the two other types. Fearful avoidants tend to crave closeness and connection but simultaneously feel uncomfortable with it.

This can be really confusing for you and for other people. As a fearful avoidant, you might genuinely want closer friendships but end up pushing friends away when they get too close. You're basically in a tug-of-war with yourself where you act anxiously attached sometimes and dismissively attached at other times.

This attachment style comes from unreliable parenting, just like the anxious style. The difference is that with anxious attachment, the caregivers are sometimes a source of comfort and sometimes not. With fearful avoidant attachment, the caregivers are comforting sometimes and scary at other times. This is where "fearful" comes in.

If you're a fearful avoidant, your parents might have been safe sources of comfort on some occasions and lash out, yell, or threaten you at other times. You couldn't consistently rely on your parents to be comforting because they were also a source of fear and danger. You might have grown up being nervous about "which version" of your parents you would get at any given time.

This causes the people-pleasing behaviors of the anxious style because you start catering to the caregiver to protect yourself from harm. This is why people-pleasing is a trauma-based version of the fight-or-flight response: the *fawn* response. This response involves using people-pleasing to deal with impending danger. You may have learned that your caregiver will be less dangerous if you placate them as soon as they get home, for example.

However, it also causes avoiding behaviors, too. This parenting style teaches you that people are inherently dangerous—even when they seem safe and caring. It results in adults that crave the closeness they were seeking as a child but feel too unsafe and worried to ever fully appreciate it.

This is the most stressful attachment style to have because it means that you're avoiding what you really want. You're choosing to be alone because it feels safer—even though you crave something else.

STOP THE CYCLE

How do you change the way you relate to other people?

All attachment styles are just learned behaviors. They're how you learned to survive your upbringing and early experiences. Due to that, a lot of our attachment issues stem from a feeling that we aren't safe or that we're responsible for everyone else.

You might be a grown adult walking around in your life feeling constantly unsafe. I know I was! The thing is, you're an adult now. You don't have to wait for someone else to make you feel safe. You can do it for yourself.

Yes, there are still weirdos out there; yes, carrying that pepper spray is still probably a good idea, but you shouldn't have to worry that being your true self is going to be dangerous anymore. If your friends make you feel unsafe, *stop being their friends.*

Learn to have faith in yourself and your own voice. You deserve a life that genuinely serves you and makes you happy. What other people think of you doesn't matter as much as you think that it does.

Do you crave close connections with people? Those connections are born when you start being honest about how you really feel. The same is true if you just need a little space.

A BADASS CHECK-IN

Learning about attachments is an incredibly important step on the way to becoming your truest, most badass self. It'll help you understand your first impulses, so you can decide if you want to act on them or not. You can see how your attachment style relates to other people and manage your relationships more confidently.

This knowledge is even more helpful when you combine it with what you learned in Chapter 2 and 3. Your attachment style is part of why these things are holding you back, and understanding it will help you understand your behavior a little better, too. It'll help you learn what you really want and how to share that effectively with other people.

Opening up and being vulnerable with other people is really hard, but it's one of the only ways that you can finally feel better and make your life your own. Making that change all starts by quieting the inner critic that says you aren't good enough, so that's what we'll get into in the next chapter.

6

SHUT UP THAT LITTLE VOICE

You've learned about why you hold certain core beliefs, where they come from, and how they affect your relationships. Armed with all that knowledge, you're ready to start changing your life!

As you've learned in the previous chapters, your experiences can make a world of difference. That's also true when it comes to healing. So, depending on your limiting beliefs and thoughts, you'll find different healing styles helpful. In this chapter, we'll go through a bunch of strategies that might benefit you. Feel free to take the ones that work and leave the ones that don't.

Now, we'll dig into each technique and how to use it. You'll finally shut up that inner critic once and for all!

POSITIVE SELF-TALK

You knew I was going here, right? Yes, this is an obvious one, but it's also something that so many people *don't do*. Stop self-sabotaging by bringing yourself down all the time!

Here's how you do it:

1. Catch yourself engaging in negative self-talk. When you notice that you're badmouthing yourself, take note. This might take some time to master, and you might only notice after you've already been doing it for a while. That's okay; you just have to start catching yourself earlier.

2. Stop it! As soon as you notice it, interrupt the thought and apologize to yourself. It sounds silly, but it really helps. Something like, "That was unfair of me, and I want to stop doing that." It doesn't even have to include the word "sorry" if it makes you feel weird.

3. Replace the negative thought with a positive counterpart. Immediately tell yourself something positive to replace the negative. Say it out loud multiple times for the best results. For example, if you caught yourself saying, "I look awful today," replace it with, "I have a great smile," or even, "My appearance doesn't determine my value." Replacing a negative statement with its exact opposite can feel more than a little forced, so you don't have to respond to, "I'm ugly" with, "No, I'm beautiful!" Instead, try saying something positive about yourself that feels believable in that moment.

Neutrality

You might feel weird telling yourself how great you are, especially if you're used to berating yourself. If positive statements feel fake, try something more approachable: neutrality.

You probably believe that everyone in the world has some inherent value just for being a person. The people you walk by on the street don't have to do anything special to deserve their life and to not hate themselves. They're just people.

Well, what about putting yourself into that mix?

You're also a person who deserves basic human decency. No one deserves to have a bully following them around 24/7, and you don't, either.

If saying, "I'm a good person who deserves good things" makes you want to barf, try this: "I'm a person like everyone else, and I deserve basic human decency just like everyone else."

Positive self-talk doesn't mean that you have to blather on in your head about how great you are, especially if it feels wrong to you. Just try to be a little easier on yourself.

Negative Narratives

If you've got less of a, "I say bad stuff about myself" vibe and more of a, "I tell myself this story that I'm an evil wench" vibe, this is for you.

Positive self-talk is also helpful when you have a constant stream of negativity connected to a bad inner story. If your story is that you are inherently bad, you probably use every excuse you can to remind yourself of that. Well, you can use the same strategy to change it. It's a similar process to what we did in the last section.

The only difference is that you'll probably be doing this a lot more since your negative narrative is more ingrained than negative self-talk. Anytime you have a negative thought about yourself, you want to counter the thought *and* the negative narrative behind it. If the story you're holding on to says, "I am inherently bad, and everything I do is wrong," reject that story every single time you correct a negative thought.

For example, you might think, *Ugh, I messed up again. I can't do anything right.* You would counter this with something like, *Everyone makes mistakes, so I'm just as good as everyone else. I'm okay.* Simply adding that little "I'm okay" reminds you that you aren't bad; you're just normal. It will help you release the negative narrative you've been telling yourself.

RELEASING NEGATIVE EMOTIONS

If you aren't super into talking to yourself, I've got another option for you. Instead of trying to turn negative thoughts into positive ones, you can find ways to release the negative energy that you've been struggling with.

Exercise

Exercise can be a great outlet for negative energy. It can help you to wear yourself out when you're feeling worked up. It's basically the same thing as taking a kid to the park, so they won't be bouncing off the walls all day—except you're more transparent about the whole thing than you would be with a kid.

That's why it can be such a great form of self-care: You know that you're exercising to make things easier on yourself later. It might be hard in the moment, but it will help you to work through your feelings and relax afterward. At its heart, that's what good self-care is.

Depending on how active you are and how worked up you are, you might choose different types of exercise. Doing cardio might help you burn off anger, but you might choose yoga when you're anxious. Going on a walk outside is a good option, too. You don't have to do an intense workout to burn off the bad vibes. Anything helps!

Write It Out

If exercising isn't your thing, writing might help you find some clarity. Journaling is a great option, and you can use prompts or try freewriting about your thoughts.

Journaling can be intimidating for some of us. You might feel like you have to write something pretty and nice to warrant having it written down in a little book.

You can try this instead: junk-dumping. This is my personal term for any kind of writing that you don't want to keep. You just write on an "impermanent" surface like a dry-erase board, chalkboard, or scraps of paper you're going to toss. You can even type up a note on your phone and delete it immediately after.

The point is just to get your feeling out. They don't have to look pretty because no one (including you) is going to look at them again. It won't be memorialized forever in a notebook; it's just a scrap of paper you're about to tear to shreds or a document that will be deleted.

It's such a freeing way to journal because you can say whatever is on your mind without any kind of filter. This can help you release a lot of tension, especially if you have a lot of frustration or resentment that you don't really want to share with people in your life (or anyone who finds your journal).

If you want to take it one step further, destroying the junk can be part of the healing process, too—especially if you're sharing worries or feelings you don't want to deal with. Writing out those feelings releases them from your body and mind. When you erase them or tear them up, you're completely free of them. It's basically free therapy.

SELF-COMPASSION

You probably think you know what self-care looks like. If you've ever been on Pinterest or bought a face mask, you know what I'm talking about. In theory, self-care is pampering yourself by doing things that help you relax, unwind, and feel better. Sometimes, that works! Bubble baths can be relaxing, and sometimes, a day at the spa really is what you need.

The thing is, these "self-care" behaviors aren't always helpful in the long run. You might feel nice in the moment, but how do you feel afterward?

You probably end up stressed about how much money you spent or worried about all the stuff you still have to get done.

Overall, you're worse off than if you didn't self-care. Weird, right?

That's the problem with stereotypical self-care. It encourages a "treat yourself" attitude that makes you feel better for an hour but doesn't solve your problem. It usually makes your problem worse by encouraging you to ignore it and delay the consequences.

So what does real self-care look like?

Working for Your Future Self

Self-care isn't always fun or relaxing. It can feel pretty bad when you're doing it, but you'll know that it's self-care because it *helps you feel better later.* It might involve taking inventory of every-thing you need to do this week and doing extra work today, so you can take Saturday off. It might mean cleaning the kitchen on the weekend, so it doesn't stress you out all week.

Self-care might be making plans with friends when you want to chill at home because being home alone makes you sad. It's all about finding creative solutions to the things that stress you out and make you feel worse.

At its core, self-care is just doing work for your future self. You're thinking about what you'll be dealing with later and what you can do now to make that easier. Once you get into this habit, your life will get easier. You won't have to do as much to keep your future self from suffering because you prepared for it last week. It starts a snowball effect where you get more organized and have more time to relax when you need it.

Judging Yourself Less

You might not consider yourself a judgmental person, but I bet you're incredibly judgmental of yourself. Most of us are our own worst critic, after all. So, if your first thought when you make a mistake is, *I'm such an embarrassment,* think about that!

This ties in with negative self-talk and negative narratives, but it's a huge part of self-care. How can you feel taken care of, loved, and supported by yourself when you're bullying yourself in your head?

So, when you make a mistake, try to be gentle with yourself. Treat yourself with kindness and respect. It's what you deserve.

You Don't Have to Give Up Bubble Baths

If you're worried that this new form of self-care sounds like a bad time, here's some good news: You don't have to give up on all the other types of self-care that you love!

Incorporating more practical self-love strategies doesn't mean you can't indulge. In fact, it might give you more time to relax in the long run. Just save your indulgent self-care for after you've done the practical stuff. That way, you'll actually be able to relax. You won't have all the things you need to do rattling around in your brain.

If more expensive self-care treatments are your style, part of your practical self-care strategy could be budgeting. You can budget out how much money you need for rent, utilities, food, and every-thing else. If you stick to your budget, you'll know that you can afford that pampering treatment or spa day you really want.

No matter what your favorite kind of pampering is, you still can (and should) enjoy it. Just plan ahead to make sure you can do it right, so it isn't weighing on your conscience the whole time.

REPARENTING

If your parents were less than ideal, you might benefit from **reparenting.** Reparenting is basically being your own parent. It doesn't mean cutting off contact with your parents or anything like that. It's doing little things to take care of yourself and feel loved.

Reparenting is the extreme sport version of self-care. You can think about it like taking care of your younger self who went without the attention, love, or support that she needed. It's one step above looking out for your current needs because you're paying attention to why those needs, and feelings are there. You notice when negative feelings come up and how they connect with your younger self.

Maybe you feel anxious in social situations because you were bullied as a kid. When you notice those feelings, you can have empathy for your younger self who doesn't want to be bullied again. Think about what would calm down that version of you who feels unsafe.

Maybe you'll want to excuse yourself for five minutes to get some fresh air and remind yourself that everything is okay. Some people will bring a small comfort object in their purse to help soothe their younger self. This could be as simple as bringing some lavender oil to smell when you get stressed out—an object that always soothed you as a kid.

You can apply this strategy to any situation. Whenever you start to feel overwhelmed with feelings, especially if they feel irrational to you, try to tune in to your younger self. What is she feeling at this moment? Why is she feeling it?

This is an amazing way to start feeling empathy for yourself and understand your emotions. It can help to have that distance from your current self. Plus, it's always easier to feel empathy for a young kid who didn't know any better.

Remember that, in some ways, you still are that kid. You might be an adult now who can handle things yourself, but you're an adult with your childhood self tucked inside you. You still carry her everywhere; you just can't let her run the show anymore.

Whenever you start to think negatively about yourself, keep that in mind. You've accomplished everything in your life with a screaming child on your back. If you've done that literally as well as figuratively, more props to you!

Some other reparenting techniques include:

- Maintaining healthy boundaries that make your inner child feel safe
- Cooking your childhood favorite foods
- Getting or doing something you always wanted as a kid
- Giving yourself rewards for doing hard things
- Correcting negative self-talk
- Writing letters to your younger self (or to your current self from your younger self)
- Being loving and kind to yourself as you would to a child
- Doing childhood favorite activities (coloring, playing, dancing, reading)

Reparenting can help you release a lot of the pain you might feel if you missed out on a good childhood. It's a great option that helps you build trust and connection with yourself while recovering from your past.

A BADASS CHECK-IN

In this chapter, you learned how to use your inner voice for good, not evil. Instead of berating yourself, judging yourself, or constantly pushing yourself, you've been learning to respect your needs and take care of yourself in a new way.

Instead of just indulging in face masks and pedicures, you realized that self-care can be *work*. It isn't always fun to take care of yourself, but it helps you remember that you care about your emotions and your future.

Shutting up your inner critic is a long process, and you're probably not finished yet. Continuing to do activities that honor your needs (both physical and emotional) and saying kind things to yourself are important.

You can't find your inner badass when you're constantly tearing yourself down!

7

HOW TO FIGURE OUT WHAT YOU WANT

S o many women feel like their dreams are completely unattainable, but that's not true! This chapter will help you realize what you really want, so you can build up the courage to do it.

After all, it's common to be confused about what we want for our lives. You might feel torn in multiple directions at once and overwhelmed by what other people expect of you.

It's even more complicated when you start thinking about what society is expecting of you. Did you go into the humanities because you felt like you couldn't succeed in science, technology, engineering, and mathematics (STEM)? Did you water down or even ignore your dreams to do something more normal or attainable? What made you hold yourself back? It can feel like so many of your decisions weren't really your own.

That's why I'm challenging you to dig deep into your psyche and pull out the dreams and ambitions you've tucked away. Whether you're 20 or 70, there's still time for you to go after what you want.

That doesn't just apply to your career, either. After all, your career is only one of so many aspects of your life. You can be perfectly satisfied with your career but still have other areas of your life that need some extra TLC.

In general, there are four major areas of your life: growth, health, environment, and people (Mitchell, 2018). Under those umbrellas, you might have different values depending on how you spend your time, who you spend it with, and so on.

Usually, we'll have some areas that get more attention at the expense of others. You might love your job and have a great family but not feel connected with your community as a whole. Alternatively, maybe your work life is suffering because you put all the focus on what's going on at home.

Write down the aspects of your life that are important to you and how they compare to each other. Do you focus too much on physical health and not enough on emotional health?

As you balance these areas out, other areas will naturally fall into place. You might be overcompensating in some areas to make up for a lack in others. For example, you're always taking overtime because you haven't kept in touch with your friends, so there's nothing to do after work. If you're struggling with your mental health, you might not have the energy to spend on anything else.

Recognizing the parts of your life that have been neglected, whatever they might be for you, can help you decide what you need to change to start feeling better.

The process can be daunting, but so much of it is about keeping a positive attitude. I know, I know: *ugh*… but hear me out.

HOW TO BE GENUINELY POSITIVE WITHOUT FAKING IT

You don't need to see the best in everything to succeed in life. You're allowed to be a grump if you want to.

The thing is, there's a difference between being realistic and being bitter. Although bitterness can feel satisfying in the moment, it doesn't do you any favors. It primes you to expect the worst, which might lead to less disappointment. However, it also means that you aren't seeing all the possibilities that are available to you.

See Yourself Differently

The reason that positivity feels fake to you is because you're so used to seeing everything in a negative light. Optimism doesn't make sense to you anymore, so you assume that anything positive is sarcastic or "just being nice." Sure, the world might not be making your dreams come true just yet, but that doesn't mean there's something wrong with you. You're still just as capable, strong, and smart as you always have been—no matter where you are now. If you want to be bitter about the state of the world, I don't blame you. Just don't be bitter about yourself.

See, when you're feeling downtrodden, you'll start thinking in negatives. *I can't do this, All I do is fail,* and *I should just give up* are common thoughts, but they only make us feel less capable and make us less likely to try next time.

Imagine that you failed a big test. When you got the grade back, you told yourself how embarrassing it was and how much of a failure you are. You had a hard time studying for the retest because you were so worried that you would fail again. You fell into bad coping mechanisms like drinking or procrastinating; suddenly, it was exam day again, and you weren't prepared. You felt totally stressed out and knew that you were going to fail again. When you received another failing grade, you gave up on the test altogether.

What if this happened instead: You still failed that big test, but when you got the grade back, you remembered that you hadn't studied properly. You decided that you would work hard and pass it this time, so you made a study schedule with planned breaks, so you wouldn't get as stressed out. By sticking to your schedule and being kind to yourself, you made studying for the retest way less stressful. When you walked into the exam for the retake, you knew you could do better than last time. This time, you finally passed.

That's how much your perspective changes the game! The unfortunate truth is that we tend to attract what we're thinking about. When you're overly worried, bullying yourself for failing, and expecting to do poorly, you're encouraging that outcome.

Expecting to do poorly will make you feel incompetent, sad, and anxious. You might think that feeling guilty about your performance will make you perform better, but that isn't exactly true. All of that stress can be paralyzing. At best, it will make it hard to focus on your studies as you wrestle with guilt and anxiety. At worst, it will make you want to give up because you feel like you can't do it either way.

This has been proven time and time again by researchers. One of my favorite examples is a study of self-determined luck. This study (Chu, 2018) focused on the difference between people who considered themselves lucky and unlucky. It turns out that there are huge differences in personality, test performance, and life satisfaction between the two groups.

Lucky people were more likely to notice small details, complete tasks faster, and be open to opportunities (Chu, 2018). One of the main differences was a higher neuroticism score in self-proclaimed unlucky people, whose anxiety might have made it hard to finish tasks as quickly or notice smaller details.

This anxiety was also in contrast to the lucky person's sociability, which made them more likely to smile and interact with new people. Being social helped the lucky people generate more opportunities because they spoke to more people and could find out about more options. In contrast, unlucky people were more likely to speak to only one or two people and miss out on the wide variety of opportunities that were available.

Surprisingly, the lucky person's optimism was a huge source of their luck. Even in bad situations, they felt lucky because they were able to see the positives. Meanwhile, unlucky people would only point out the negatives and feel unlucky in the same scenario.

Luckily (see what I did there?), you don't have to be unlucky for life. Researchers in the same study found that unlucky people were able to become lucky, and lucky people could become luckier with a few simple teachings (Chu, 2018). Try them out yourself to feel luckier:

- Try something new: Changing up your routine can open you to new opportunities. When you do the same thing all the time, there's no chance for something better to come along! Trying new things gives luck an opportunity to sneak into your life.
- See the good: Gratitude can give you a huge perspective shift. You might not go from a pessimist to an optimist overnight, but you can start to notice the good things about yourself and your life. Enjoy and appreciate them —even if they feel small.
- Be open-minded: Don't use tunnel vision on a goal so much that you miss out on other opportunities. Be open to new chances that could be even better. This will only make you more dedicated in the long run because you'll be open to new and better opportunities if you find them. If your plans don't change, you'll know that you're on the best path for you right now.

Using these techniques is a great way to improve your view of yourself and your life. It helps you recognize and appreciate the opportunities that are available to you. You're capable of so much more than you realize!

The Possible You

With that in mind, there are bound to be possibilities that you don't know about yet. How can you realize your potential when you don't even know what's out there? Exploration is a huge help. Trying new things will help you realize all the opportunities around you. The more that you do, the more you'll find where you belong.

You probably feel like some possibilities are already off-limits and that you're not young, fit, or smart enough to do them. We'll go through this later and see what's really not possible, so put that on hold for a second. Before you start discounting all of your desires, give yourself room to dream. What would your ideal self be like?

If anything was possible, what would you want to do with your life? How would you spend your time?

Write or type out a list with everything that comes to mind. At this point, don't try to make a succinct list. Write down as much as you can. You might have multiple versions of your ideal self, and that's awesome! To keep better track of them, you can keep separate lists of what each version would be like. Alternatively, put them together, so you can pick your favorite parts from each.

This is your possibility list! It's a collection of all the things you could do in your life. You can include everything from restaurants you want to eat at to careers, companies, or foundations you want to build. No dream is too big or small to go on your list. Maybe you have always wanted to learn to knit, paint, play pickleball, run a marathon, or skydive! Anything that makes you feel a little jolt of joy and excitement is worth writing down.

You'll be keeping this list for the foreseeable future, so don't worry about what you might be missing. You can always add to it later. Some great things to include are:

- Career options
- Business/side hustle ideas
- Charities you want to form or work with
- Hobbies you already love
- Activities you want to try
- Events you want to attend
- People you want to get to know better
- Places you want to visit

Organize it into as many categories as you want. Color-code to your heart's content or just shove everything into one big list. Whatever works for you is fine as long as you have a list full of possibilities for your life.

If you're having trouble coming up with a list, don't worry. This next exercise will help with that.

Meditation: A Meeting With Your Future Self

To get past mental blocks and discover who you really want to be, try this meditation. You don't have to be experienced with meditation to benefit from this exercise.

Find a comfortable position—either sitting or lying down. Take inventory of your body. Are your muscles tight? Are you clenching your jaw? Spend a moment readjusting your body, releasing tension, and relaxing. If you want to, feel free to give any especially tense areas a little massage.

Now that you're feeling more comfortable, take a deep breath in and close your eyes. Hold it for one second before slowly releasing it. Do this four more times. If any thoughts come up, try to notice them without judgment. See them like clouds passing by in the sky—parts of your experience but not defining parts of you.

Imagine that you can see your ideal future self in the distance. She's the person you want to be in 10, 20, or even 30 years.

What does she look like? Is she wearing simple or extravagant clothing, and how is her hair styled? What does her expression look like? Spend a few minutes filling in the details about her appearance.

Where are you imagining her? Is she in her home, at work, or in another place entirely?

What do those details say about her lifestyle? Is she busy and perfectionistic or relaxed and laid back? What does she do in her spare time? Does she have pets, children, or loved ones around her? Allow yourself to fully imagine the scene. You can spend as long as you like filling in the details. Then, it's time to speak to her.

You can ask your future self anything that you want. She already knows what you're going through because she's been through it. She won't be shocked or judge you for anything you have to say. Best of all, she knows exactly what you need to hear right now.

Imagine yourself asking her whatever has been troubling you. What's been on your mind recently? What do you desperately need advice on?

Once you've asked your questions, think deeply about how your future self would respond. What advice would a wiser version of you have to offer? Did she make a mistake and learn from it? How would she navigate your situation?

When you have your answer, you're free to start coming back. Thank your future self for her help, and feel gratitude wash over you as you return to your normal life with this advice.

Open your eyes.

Making Fantasy Into Reality

Now that you've finished your meditation, you should have a

better idea of who you want to become. You've also got a clearer concept of how your future self thinks and what she values.

Of course, this is all an exercise in imagination, but it can really help. It can make it easier to picture who you genuinely want to become.

Is there anything from the meditation that wasn't on your list? Add it in now. This meditation often brings up ideas that we never thought about before, and it's a great way to add more options to our list of possibilities.

Delve into that list again. If you had infinite time and money, what would you do all day?

At this point, you aren't trying to narrow down your list. We want to make it as big as possible, so you can see every option available to you. This covers anything you might want to be, do, or try, including things you already love and do all the time and things you've never done before.

So Who Could You Be?

The items on your list are the life possibilities that you care about right now. There are probably a lot more than you expected, right?

Avoid the instinct to tell yourself that certain options are off-limits or unattainable for some reason. There are always alternative ways to make your goals happen, so just let them be for now.

Do you see how many other options there are? You don't have to feel stuck anymore. There are so many different and better ways of living your life.

What items on your list make you the most excited? Are there things you're dying to try or that you would love to spend all day doing?

These are the things that should be taking up the precious time and space in your life. You might already know some things that you want to build your life around but keep your mind and heart open to other possibilities until you've tried everything from your list. We'll be doing that in the next chapter!

For now, just notice the things that excite you. What sort of things make you joyful? Are there certain activities or hobbies that never make your list? If you want to take it one step further, you can take note of certain categories that tend to add to your life and ones that tend to take away from it. This can help you add even more options to your list for later.

Keeping this possibility list will help in two major ways. Obviously, it'll help you remember how many possibilities are available to you. It will remind you that you do have options, and you aren't stuck. You can't tell yourself that lie when you already have a whole list of them, after all!

Second, this list will help you stay open-minded and keep trying new things. There are probably tons of items on your list that you've never tried before, and it's important to push yourself to try them. If you're like me, you can fall into routines pretty easily and end up doing the same thing every day. This list gives you a quick way out of that with lots of new options to try. Add to your list any moment you think of another possibility that interests you.

Who You Aren't

We only want to remove things from your list that you don't like. Is anything on your list there because you feel like it *should* be there?

You might feel obligated to keep doing your work, a type of exercise, or something else that you know deep down isn't really you.

If you imagine your buff future self working out all the time while you hate working out, you might have to reimagine that. It doesn't mean that you won't achieve that goal, but you might live that dream in a different way, like doing a workout that you like better or working out less regularly.

Are there any items on your list just because people expect them to be there? After a while, it can be hard to tell the difference between who we are and who other people say we are. Be careful to make that distinction. If you aren't sure, take note of that beside the point on your list. Then you'll know to keep thinking about it as you move forward.

There might be some aspects of your current life that didn't make your list. Is there anything you spend a lot of time on right now that you don't enjoy as much as you thought? That's also something to pay attention to!

What's Impossible?

If you feel like one of the possibilities on your list is impossible, think long and hard about if that's true. Are you discounting your abilities or falling prey to stereotypes? You might feel like you're too old to change careers at 30, but that's just a stereotype. If you have the capability, time, and willpower to do something you'll love, why not?

Sometimes, one of your favorite possibilities will be genuinely impossible. It might be because of physical or mental health limitations, money, time restraints, family, or something else. It can be hard to acknowledge, especially if it's something you've always wanted.

One way to deal with it is compromise. Is there some way you can make this dream happen—even if it's not exactly the same? Do some research into your situation and see if there's an alternative way to make it work.

There might be something similar that will make you happy. You might not have the money, time, or energy to go to medical school and become a doctor, but you could get a job in a hospital transporting patients or bringing them food. Maybe you can't get exactly what you want, but you can get close enough to the dream that you'll be satisfied.

Alternatively, you might choose to go after another goal entirely. Being close to your dream job but not quite achieving it could be frustrating, and it isn't for everyone. Instead, you might go after another dream job in a completely different field. Have faith that you're doing what you were meant for and to go after what feels right to you.

The Positivity Effect

Are you starting to see the benefits of positive thinking? It's shocking to see how much a positive outlook can change your life.

You've spent such a long time convincing yourself that you can't, believing that you weren't capable or deserving of change. Most of us have been through things that would make it easy to stay down. You might've let the bad stuff pile up on you until you couldn't move at all. When you have help shoveling it all off, it gets so much easier.

There are so many opportunities waiting for you, but you've been blind to them for so long. How does it feel to have them back in sight? Let's see just how different your life can be when you start believing in all your possibilities. I hope that you feel luckier and more capable than you ever have.

A BADASS CHECK-IN

Before you read this chapter, you might have felt like positive thinking was just a New Age myth. I hope you're starting to see just how powerful it can be!

In the last few chapters, you learned a lot about what *not* to do.

It can be hard to make progress when you have nothing to replace those negative thoughts with. Well, now you know how to do that!

Positive thinking is a crucial aspect of being a badass. It means believing in yourself—even when no one else does. It means that you have hope for the future, and you never give up on your dreams. It might sound cheesy, but it's true. You can't accomplish all the things that your badass self wants (and deserves) when you don't believe in yourself and what you're capable of.

I hope that your dreams are becoming even clearer. Most of all, I hope that you're getting the courage to pursue them!

8

STARTING OUT

Now that you have an idea of who you want to be, it's time to start making it happen! Let's explore your options and figure out what's right for you.

The idea you have of your ideal self is probably pretty vague right now. You have a list of things you might like to do, but it isn't set in stone yet. That's great! You don't want to write your future in permanent ink before you've explored all possible avenues. You want to know way more about yourself before you make that kind of commitment.

This is the perfect time to start trying stuff! Start looking into your passions and open yourself up to everything you want to try.

Side Note: If you haven't already, this would be a great time to try my workbook! It has tons of exercises to help you figure out what you want and become your most badass self. It's the perfect companion to this book and will help you to process everything you've been learning here. Grab your copy for free! You can find the link at the end of the conclusion.

The exercises in the workbook will help you delve more deeply into the topics we cover and get the most out of all the work you're doing to improve your life. I recommend starting it now before we get too far along in the process!

TRY STUFF!

It's time to start experimenting with items from your list. In your free time, try out some of the options and see how they feel!

Some might be easier to try than others. You can't exactly start a new career out of nowhere. Instead, you can try learning more about that career path and what that sort of work would be like. Watch day-in-the-life videos and practice doing similar things. How does it feel to do that kind of work? Would you enjoy that day-to-day?

For simpler options, it will be a lot easier to tell if you like them. Going swimming, playing baseball, or eating new food are easy to arrange.

Regardless of the activity you're trying, keep track of how you felt about it. You might have to try each thing a few times to get a feel for what it's really like.

HOW TO KEEP A JOURNAL

Keeping a journal is one of the easiest ways to keep track of what you've tried and how you felt about it. You might feel like it's a daunting task, but it doesn't have to be. Below are my journaling tips for you.

Don't Use a Real Book (Unless You Want To)

You might think that you need to have a beautiful, physical record of your thoughts to keep a journal, but that's not true. You don't need to use something pretty. In fact, you don't need to use a real book at all.

If physically writing things down works for you, go ahead and use a notebook. If buying a pretty journal will make you more motivated to write, do it! If you look at a blank notebook and feel pure dread, another route might be better for you.

A lot of people feel overwhelmed by the blankness of a new journal, especially a pretty one. If that's you, then you don't need to use one! If you have a half-used school notebook, you can just use the last half as your journal. You can even write on loose-leaf paper or on the back of an old bill or school assignment. It doesn't have to be pretty as long as you can keep it all together. You can do that by tucking everything into a binder or folder.

Unlike for negative thought journaling, you will want to keep a record of your feelings here. This is how you'll remember what you tried and how it made you feel. If you do end up writing on bits of scrap, make sure you have a way to keep them all together.

If physically writing doesn't work for you, no problem! There are tons of options for online journals. You can keep a record of your thoughts in a document, in the notes on your phone, or even make a private blog about it.

If you like to keep your entries separate (rather than having everything in one document), you can keep a folder of dated documents or opt for a note-taking app instead. Note-taking apps are designed to have sections upon sections, so you can categorize based on what you're trying and the date. You can even color-code the tabs to represent different emotions, so you can see, at a glance, how you felt about each one.

Don't Write on the First Page

If you want to keep a physical journal but feel intimidated by that blank first page, this is for you: Just leave the first page empty when you start! This way, you can get started immediately without worrying as much about "ruining" that first page. You don't have to deal with writing the perfect first entry. You're just starting now, and you can fill in the first page when you're ready.

Personally, I often leave the first page blank until I've filled out the entire book. I might go back and make a collage or collection of quotes there that represent what I felt and learned throughout the process. Or, I'll add in thoughts, song lyrics, or quotes there as I go along. You might want to draw something on the first page later on, too. Fill it in as you go; you do what works for you.

Don't Sweat the Grammatical Stuff

Don't worry about writing in your best cursive with perfect grammar and sentence structure. The only person who will read this is you, so it doesn't have to be pretty. Remember: This is your journal, so it doesn't have to meet any requirements except for yours. Feel free to:

- write in point form,
- write in sentence fragments,
- curse as much as you want,
- start a sentence and not finish it,
- rant,
- change pen colors mid-sentence,
- make doodles instead of writing, or
- make an entry with just one or two words... or 2,000 words.

All the pressure you feel about keeping a journal probably comes from school. We've all had that assignment where we had to keep a journal, and our teacher would grade us on it. Maybe you had a nosy sister or parent who kept reading your diary as a kid.

Well, not to worry: This one is safe from all of those people. It's just for you, so make it a space for you to unabashedly express yourself.

What to Include

The point of this journal is to keep a record of how you feel after trying each item from your possibility list. Some things you might want to keep track of are:

- how you felt doing it (in the moment),
- how you felt after doing it,
- if you want to do it again,
- anything that could have influenced your experience, or
- your final rating.

I recommend making at least three entries for each one before you decide against a possibility. If you feel 100% sure you never want to do it again, take another look at the factors that influenced your experience. Would they be the same if you went again? Would it be worth it to find a way to enjoy this activity, or is it more trouble than it's worth?

If you know right away that something isn't for you, don't feel pressured to suffer through multiple tries. Just keep an open mind, and you might find something else to include on your list instead!

Getting Out of Your Comfort Zone

You've learned how to keep track of the activities you want to try out, but how do you go about doing them?

You have to muster up enough bravery to try one thing. When you're starting out, try something that isn't as intimidating for you. Then, move on to the next thing and the next. As you go on, it'll get easier to tackle new things.

One great way to get out of your comfort zone is volunteering. It'll expose you to new ideas and experiences you might have never had before, all while you're helping out your community. You'll have the added comfort of being around like-minded people plus a team of coordinators who are there to support you. It's an awesome way to ease yourself into trying something new!

If you feel nervous about trying one of the items on your list, why is that? What in particular about that activity scares you? Are you worried about being judged by others or about not knowing how things work?

You can minimize these stresses by inviting a friend or family member to go with you. It's easier to mess up and look silly when you have someone you trust to look silly with you. You can also look up reviews online to get a feel for how different places operate. If there's anything out of the ordinary about the place you'll be going, you'll probably hear about it in the reviews.

For example, if you plan on going swimming, you might see people in the reviews mention that they hate when people leave their shoes on in the changing room. If you're nervous about going, knowing about this custom ahead of time can make you feel more ready. In reality, people probably won't care if you do these things or not. It's just an exercise to help you feel more comfortable and prepared, so only do it if you want to.

If you still feel overwhelmed by any of your activities, it can be hard to tell if it's a good challenge or a real threat to your well-being. Sometimes, it's hard to start something that will be amazing for you in the long term but being difficult doesn't always mean something is good for you!

If you haven't tried the activity at all, I recommend finding a way to ease into it before making a final decision. Bring a friend; call ahead and ask for information; or stake out the area before you go. Be prepared to cut your first attempt short if it's too intense for you.

The whole point of this exercise is to try things you might love, so you need to give yourself time to adjust to the experience. Most things are more stressful to think about than to do. Similarly, the first time will be more stressful than each time after that.

One great way to prepare is to think about the likelihood of the worst possible outcome. After all, what you're worried about is probably the worst thing that could happen. What are the chances of that happening? What is most likely to happen instead? I bet you'd feel less stressed worrying about the most likely scenario instead! Remind yourself that feeling nervous before new experiences is normal. You're going to feel nervous, and then it'll go away. You can handle it!

It can help to think about what you would do if the worst possible scenario did happen. What if you went to that event and everyone you know suddenly hated you? You could try to enjoy it by yourself or cut the night short and take yourself out for ice cream. This can help you realize that even the worst possible scenario isn't that bad, and it's also very unlikely. No matter what happens, you're going to be okay.

Your anxiety might be about some aspect of the activity that you can't prepare for. It might not go down—no matter how much planning you do. If it's unbearable, you might need to build up slowly to try this possibility out. That's fine! You might have a second tier of possibilities that you'll try once you're more comfortable.

In general, you should trust your instincts about things like this. If you aren't 100% sure if something is a good idea for you, don't do it just yet. Feel free to go home early, not participate, or cancel those plans. The key is to reevaluate later. How did you feel about *not* doing that? Did you feel relieved, guilty, or disappointed that you missed out? Get in tune with that feeling. Are you glad that you didn't participate, or do you want to try again?

This is a great rule of thumb because it helps you navigate all the confusing emotions that can come when an event is upcoming. You can learn pretty quickly what you feel nervous about but enjoy in the long run versus what is actually dangerous for you.

As you get more confident trying new things, you might be more willing to take that risk. You'll come to understand that the danger is just feeling more anxious or needing to take a breather, but it lets you have more experiences. That's your choice to make, but just make sure that you're taking care of your safety first.

Learning Boundaries

If you're still having trouble making that choice, it can help to think about your boundaries. You can tell where your boundaries are based on where you feel squeamish or resentful (Selva, 2018). So, if trying something new makes you feel anxious, that's probably fine. But, if it makes you feel sick to your stomach or resentful, you shouldn't do it. That includes feeling so nervous that you feel sick.

As you get more practiced with trying new things and being in new situations, your boundaries will get clearer. This definition of a boundary can be applied to almost anything, so it's a great way to start out. Keep in mind that your boundaries might shift over time, too.

WHAT DO YOU LOVE?

After you've spent some time trying stuff, some activities will stand out. You'll notice the stuff that you love and the stuff you never want to do again. It's time to start narrowing down that list to the things that speak to you.

Start by flipping through your journal and refreshing your memory on things you tried earlier on. Take a look at the ratings you gave each experience. Did anything get a perfect score from you? Did anything get a zero? Which things do you want to avoid in the future, and what would you do tomorrow if you could?

It'll be easiest to start with the things you weren't into.

Things You Hate

Hate might be a strong word, or it might not. Regardless, you were bound to try some things that didn't work for you. Maybe they were stressful, not feasible, or just plain boring. It'll be easy to cross the stuff you hate off your list.

Here's the thing, though: You should also cross off the things that you don't feel enthusiastic about. With all the items on your list, there are bound to be some things that you feel excited to keep doing. When you're deciding what you want to keep, it should be the things that make you *feel* something. If there are possibilities on your list that you feel "meh" about, you don't need to keep them around.

You want to make space in your life for the things that make you the happiest and most fulfilled. You don't need to keep doing activities that just aren't doing it for you. When you're deciding what you want to keep, ask yourself this question: Do I want to keep investing my time into this?

If the answer is no, cross it off with no guilt. Don't feel like you have to keep doing something just because you tried it a few times! You should be proud of yourself for exploring things that might have spoken to you. Now you know that they don't, so you aren't missing out on anything.

Things You Love

There should be at least one or two things on your list that you definitely want to do again. These are the items that jump out from your memory and get 10/10 reviews in your journal.

Which activities got rave reviews? Is there common ground between them? Noticing the connections here will help you to better understand yourself. It can also help you find other things you might want to try. You want to figure out which activities resonated with you, so you know what you want to incorporate into your life. Star or mark these items, so you can easily remember them later.

Was there anything on your list that you could see yourself doing for the rest of your life or maybe even as a career? Take note of that to dig into later!

When Everything Is Meh

If nothing on your list got a rave review, that's okay, too. It could mean that you haven't hit on something that excites you yet. You also might not be used to giving high scores, so if you tend to rate things low, take a look at the highest scores on your list.

It doesn't mean that there's something wrong with you! You've just got to reevaluate your list and try some more things.

A BADASS CHECK-IN

It can be really intimidating to start making changes in your life. Trying just one new thing can be tiring, let alone trying a bunch of things. A bad experience could put you out of commission for a week or more.

The great result of all this is that, no matter what, you'll come out of this experience with a better understanding of yourself. You can't properly stand up for yourself or follow your passions when you don't know what they are! Hopefully this chapter helped you learn where those passions might be for you.

Plus, the more you do hard things, the easier it'll get. You're inadvertently becoming super resilient just by trying a bunch of things that might or might not work out. As you try more and more, it gets easier every time. By the time you're done, doing hard things for your badass self will be easy!

GIVE YOURSELF A BREAK

If you've been following along with this book as you make changes in real life, you'll probably be feeling pretty worn out. You've been trying tons of new things and learning so much about yourself. It should be a fun experience, but that doesn't mean it isn't stressful and tiring, too.

Congratulate yourself for all your hard work! Don't worry about making progress for a week or two—or longer if you need it. Relaxing and enjoying your new hobbies will help you build a solid idea of the future you want. There might be some major changes you want to make, but you don't want to rush them. Let them solidify in your brain before you push forward. When you feel refreshed and ready to keep going, you can get started on the next chapter.

9

WRITING YOUR OWN STORY

After narrowing down your interests, you should have a better idea of what you want to pursue in the long term. Some of your goals might seem reasonable, but the bigger ones might feel hard to reach or completely unattainable. Don't worry: That's all part of the process.

In this chapter, you'll be taking a huge step by planning out what you want to spend time on in the future. The last two chapters have helped you figure out your interests, and they'll start coming to life here. You're going to write out a "life plan" that matches what you want to do as you move forward. You get to decide who you want to be!

PLAN IT OUT

This is your chance to write your own story. You can edit, erase, and rewrite your future as you please. Anything and everything in this plan is up to you. Be bold and make sure it matches what you truly want!

Before you get into the specifics, take another look at your possibility list. What's still left on it? What do you want to make into consistent hobbies? Are there any goals you want to set around them?

These questions might feel nebulous if you aren't exactly sure what you want the future to look like yet. Let's start by diving into the things you loved from your possibility list.

What Do You Want to Do?

When you think about this question, you probably start thinking about work. Our brains are trained to think about "what we do" as our career, but it doesn't have to be that way. How do you love to spend your time?

What things on your list make you the happiest? What did you put a star beside? Are these things that you want to do as a career? They may not be, but that doesn't mean they aren't worth pursuing.

If gardening made you the happiest you've ever been, you want to keep gardening regardless of what job you have. It's worth doing it consistently so that you can make a habit of it.

You want to turn your favorite activities into habits as a sneaky way of adding more fun into your life. Instead of just flopping down on the couch and watching a show, you might work in the garden for an hour first. When your hobbies are habitual, it's easier to keep them in your life.

Why It's Hard to Do Stuff You Love

Weirdly enough, it can be hard to do things—even if you love them. You might love reading, drawing, hiking, or anything else, but you just end up at home in front of a screen. It doesn't mean that there's something wrong with you or that you don't like those activities.

The screens in our lives are just really, really addicting. Games, shows, and social media are designed to be that way. That's why you have a hard time getting off your phone to do something else —even if you want to.

Some psychologists argue that the only way to fix this is to do a dopamine detox to stop feeling like screens are your main source of pleasure (Sussman, 2021). They think that by staying away from screens for a while, you can reset your reward system to find more pleasure in other activities. You'll notice how nice it feels to move your body during a brisk walk or work on a project you're passionate about.

While a dopamine detox is a great idea in a vacuum, I don't think it's practical for real life. Most of us can't stop checking our work emails—no matter how much we want to. Regardless, I think a dopamine detox is more suffering than it's worth. Life is hard enough without cutting out your screen time like you're an eight-year-old kid who just got grounded.

Here's my suggestion instead: Combine the activities you love with your screen time. For example, if you love watching online videos, try to only (or mostly) watch them when you garden. You can combine this with whatever activity you enjoy. By mixing your "high dopamine" screen activity with a real-life activity, you can find it more fun and pleasurable. It's especially effective if you get most of your screen time during that activity.

Some activities might be harder to combine with screen time. You can't exactly take a kickboxing class while watching your favorite show. Instead, just find a way to pair these activities together. Maybe you only get your favorite screen time activity after you go to that class. Keep this in mind as you go through the items on your list. Try to pair your favorite activities with dopamine-stimulating ones so that you're more likely to keep doing it.

We just went over why you should pursue things—even if you

don't want to make a career out of them. If you *do* want to make a career out of it, that deserves attention, too!

If you have any major changes that you want to make, like career changes or big life goals, you'll want to approach them with care. These big goals are more likely to seem out of reach, so you want to break them down with solid goal setting.

Good Goal Setting

A lot of our goals start off really vague. "Write a book", "eat healthy," or "get better at art" are all great ideas, but they're bad goals.

They're bad goals because they're hard to obtain, and it's hard to know when you've reached them. How do you know that you've gotten better at art? How do you know if you can cross off your goal of eating healthy? Have you written a book because you wrote a draft, or do you need a physical book in your hands?

These are the kinds of questions you want to ask yourself. Good goals should be *specific* and *attainable*. You'll know that it meets the criteria when you can definitively say that you have or have not reached it by a certain date.

Let's use getting better at art as an example. Since it's hard to quantify art improvement, you might opt to focus on practice instead. Practice will inherently make you better over time. To make it specific, you might say, "I want to practice art for an hour every day for the next year." That goal is specific, but it isn't exactly attainable (at least not for me!). To make it more doable, you could change it to, "I want to practice art for an hour every week for four months." Look into your personal schedule and time commitments and pick a goal that works for you. You don't have to spend hours a day on something to make your dream happen.

Alternatively, if your goal is based more on an achievement, you'll need to make sure you have enough time to complete it. You might opt to not set a timeline for yourself and work on the project until you complete it; alternatively, you might pick a deadline that seems reasonable at the moment and be prepared to move it if need be.

You also want to make goals more attainable by breaking them down into smaller pieces. For a big achievement like writing a novel, you might want to break it into sections. You might complete all of your research and planning by a certain date, then complete an outline by another, and write the draft by another. Breaking your goals down into chunks makes them less overwhelming and easier to achieve. Instead of feeling paralyzed by taking on a huge project, you're only handling one small portion at a time.

This strategy will help you to achieve your goals by making them achievable and breaking them down into digestible sections. This keeps you from getting in over your head with a project. You're motivated to take things one step at a time which will keep you from getting stuck halfway through.

Setting Goals for Huge Life Changes

Do you feel like you should be in a different career? You might feel resentful about your current job or just plain miserable. Maybe you've been in an unsatisfying relationship for the past 10 years. No matter what change you feel you need to make, you want it to go over as easily and painlessly as possible. I can't guarantee that your changes will be painless, but I can make them easier to handle.

The biggest question you're probably facing is this: "Should I even do this?" You might feel like the change you want will be too drastic. It will uproot your life and cause unfixable damage to your relationships. Those things might be true, but that doesn't mean you shouldn't do it.

You have to decide for yourself what you need to change to feel better. We all want to avoid doing something drastic if it isn't necessary. Some questions to ask yourself include the following:

- What is the root of the problem?: You might be stuck in a situation that you hate, but it isn't the core issue. The root of the problem is the reason why you hate it. Maybe your boss expects too much from you, you don't get paid enough, or you don't like the kind of work that you do. Take note of whatever the root of the problem is for you.
- Will this change fix the problem?: Quitting your job is fine, but do you have another job lined up that will make you happier? Will you just leave this job and end up doing something you hate more? Make sure you're changing because it will help you feel better—not just for the sake of it.
- Have I tried every other option available to me?: Drastic solutions are stressful and going through with them is difficult. If there is any other option, you might want to consider it first. Can something smaller or simpler fix this problem? For example, you might want to talk to your boss about your dissatisfaction before you quit. Could working different hours, switching departments, or something else fix the problem? Would any of those fixes make you as happy as the most drastic solution?
- Am I prepared emotionally, mentally, and physically to make this change?: Making a drastic change can involve a lot of resources. You need to be in a stable physical position and ready to handle some emotional stress. Consider your health, living situation, finances, and upcoming events. Are you prepared to go through a life change right now?

These questions are here to help you understand the scale of the changes you're making and make an informed decision. Some of them might not apply to you. If you're set on your choice, that's great.

Moving forward, you'll probably want to break this change down into several steps. The first step might involve addressing some of the questions above, like getting financially stable, finding a new place to live, or lining up a new job. Once you've done that, you can worry about the actual change, followed by whatever steps come after it.

Your big life change might not be the end goal but part of a broader picture. Once you've achieved the change, you might start working toward something else. If it's a long process, make sure that you're patient and kind to yourself. These kinds of changes are hard! You should be proud of yourself for being brave enough to do it.

You go, girl!

FACING FEAR

Making a big life change can bring up some intense feelings. You might be anxious about getting your passions wrong, making a big mistake, or not being able to achieve what you want.

Here's the truth: Everyone (yes, everyone!) feels freaked out by the prospect of a big change. People just deal with it in different ways. Even the coolest person you can think of probably feels crappy during a breakup. Instead of crying and eating ice cream, she might dive headfirst into work. Different people have different coping strategies, but that doesn't mean they aren't struggling. You aren't alone in feeling overwhelmed.

Anxiety is a normal symptom of making a big life change. There will always be a period of uncertainty and stress as you navigate your new circumstances and readjust.

I'm Making a Mistake!

If this is how you feel right now, take a deep breath. It's going to be okay: I promise.

If you haven't made any changes yet, then put your plan on hold for a while. Take some time to decide if this is what you really want before you make any decisions.

If your plan is already in motion, it might be hard to go back on it now. Depending on your circumstances, you might be able to change your mind... or you might not. If it's the latter, all hope is not lost. It's common to feel frazzled in the midst of a major life change. You might be scared of all the changes that are happening and just want things to go back to normal.

Here's the thing: People who make big life changes often end up happier than people who don't—even if the process itself is stressful (Levitt, 2020). This proves that we tend to be overly cautious about making life changes. So, if you feel like you royally screwed up, you probably didn't! You're just in a period of adjustment before you start to feel how much better things are.

If you were unhappy enough to start enacting this big life change in the first place, you probably don't want it in your life as much as you just want normalcy. When you find yourself yearning for the past, think about if you want that guy back, or that old job... or if you just want to feel normal. It's probably the latter!

Let that comfort you as you work through any big life changes. You've got this!

I Can't Do It!

If you want to make a change but feel paralyzed, lean on the questions in the last section. By answering all of them and making sure that you're prepared, you can be certain that you're making the right choice.

You can also keep the same concept in mind as the "I messed up" folks: Most people don't regret making major life changes (Levitt, 2020). If you're unhappy with your current situation, there are *so* many better options out there for you! You deserve better than a mediocre life that makes you miserable. Go out there and get what you deserve!

Positive Thoughts for Anxiety

Dealing with some major stress? Here are some things you can tell yourself to ease your mind. If you need more, flip to the next chapter!

- "I'm going to feel anxious for a while, and then I'll feel better."
- "I do what I want. Anxiety can't run my life."
- "This feeling is trying to protect me, but I don't need it right now."

These simple sayings will help remind you that anxiety isn't harmful. It's uncomfortable, but then it goes away. You can get through this.

A BADASS CHECK-IN

In this chapter, you really started to dig into your future goals— maybe for the first time. Confronting your life head-on like that isn't an easy feat, and you should be incredibly proud of yourself. Your badass self is really starting to emerge!

It's normal to deal with anxiety, second thoughts, and general unease throughout this process. You're trying to plan out a future that you can love, and there's a lot of pressure associated with that!

Just remember that no one is going to grade you on this. You're making these changes for you alone, and if they don't work out, you can try again! This isn't a limited time offer. You're always going to be the badass lady that you are, and you're always going to be capable of trying again. Don't be too hard on yourself. Every misstep is a chance to learn more about what you want and how you want to get there!

10

GIRL, HELP! I'M GETTING
WORSE!

Feeling overwhelmed? Convinced that you're going backward
and not forward?

You might feel like you've taken a huge step back and have
undone all your progress, but I promise that you haven't. With
some support, you'll be well on your way again!

DEALING WITH ANXIETY

It's normal to feel anxious when you're making a life change. It
doesn't matter if that change is moving across the country, taking
up a new hobby, or just being nicer to yourself.

Change is hard for everyone. Some of us might be more rigid
than others, but everyone has comforting routines that make them
feel better. When your routines are spun upside down, it's
stressful!

It's even harder when what's changing is you. When you're
moving houses or changing jobs, it can be a little less daunting
because you know everything else in your life will stay the same.
But, if you're moving because you want to find something more for

yourself, moving is only one step in your journey. Plus, it's not just your house that's changing. Since your mind is also growing and changing, you can feel completely out of your depth. Things that used to feel relaxing and comfortable might not feel that way anymore.

It's common to have a whole range of emotions and worries during a time like this. You might wonder if you're making any progress, if you'll be able to succeed, what the future will look like, or if it'll be worth it. You might feel confident on Friday and terrified on Sunday. It's part of the process.

Knowing that your feelings are normal should make you feel a little bit better about this. There's nothing wrong with you for feeling worried and uncomfortable. In fact, I'd be more concerned if you didn't feel anything!

When your feelings get hard to manage, focus on why you started making these changes. Why did you want this badly enough to start changing? Remind yourself why you've put in all this work and why it's important to keep fighting.

It can help to think about the progress that you've made. It's easy to focus forward, constantly moving our goalposts when we reach a goal. Don't do that! Make sure to celebrate your growth and progress—even when it's small. Doing that will help you remember how far you've come.

You are strong, smart, and capable. You've already done this much, so what's a little more to get the outcome you've been dreaming of?

If you find yourself overwhelmed by anxiety, you're not alone. Below are some tips for instant relief to get you through those tough times.

Tips for Anxiety Relief

Personifying It

It might seem weird that personifying your anxiety can make it better, but it's surprisingly effective!

If you aren't familiar with the term, personifying is pretending that a nonhuman thing is a person, so personifying your anxiety means treating it like a little person that lives in your brain.

Think about what your anxiety tells you. Does your anxiety tell you that you're not good enough? Does it tell you that situations are more dangerous than they are? Is it like a confused old lady looking out for you or more like your childhood bully?

Give your anxiety a name based on how it makes you feel and what it's trying to do.

This makes it easier to separate your anxiety from yourself. You aren't necessarily an anxious person; you've just got this annoying companion right now. It doesn't mean they'll be around forever.

This exercise can also help you recognize that your anxiety isn't exactly helping you. It's often a defense mechanism to protect us from being unsafe or exposed. Anxiety sends you into a fight-or-flight (or fawn-or-freeze) response. This primes our body to handle a stressful situation better. It's a problem because we're having this response in situations where it isn't necessary.

Being anxious might help you notice danger if you hear a twig crack in the woods, but it doesn't help you give a presentation or perform better at work.

A great thing about personifying your anxiety is that you can tell it how you're feeling. When your anxiety is ramping up before your group presentation, you can tell it that it's making your life harder. Some great ways to talk to your anxiety are:

- "I don't have time to deal with you right now. I'm going to ignore you."
- "You aren't helping me, so I'm not going to listen to you."
- "I won't let you control me!"

Grounding Yourself

Another great strategy for dealing with anxiety is to do a grounding exercise. Grounding exercises help you feel present in the current situation rather than being overwhelmed by the past or future.

If you're stressed out about something and talking to your anxiety isn't helping, try this.

My favorite grounding exercise is called the 5-4-3-2-1 technique. It's a two-minute activity that you can do anywhere to feel more present and get out of your head. It's helpful for anything from mild anxiety to a full-blown panic attack.

It's simple. Just list the following (Smith, 2018):

- Five things you can see
- Four things you can touch
- Three things you can hear
- Two things you can smell
- One thing you can taste (or a taste that you like)

This exercise gets you thinking about what's happening around you instead of what you're worrying about. It's a great distraction when you feel overwhelmed.

Belly Breathing

Belly breathing is an anxiety-reducing technique that focuses on the body and the breath. If that doesn't sound relaxing for you, feel free to skip this one.

I've found it easier to do this exercise lying down, but you can also do it sitting. You can do almost anywhere—even standing up if you need to!

Start off in a comfortable position with one hand just under your ribs and the other on your chest. On your next inhale, take in the biggest breath that you can. Imagine your lungs expanding, pushing your diaphragm down and expanding your belly. Don't push your stomach out with your stomach muscles. Let the air flowing in you and the movement of your diaphragm do the work.

Hold your breath for three seconds and then release it slowly and completely. Keep exhaling until there's no air left. Repeat this five times.

There's a common misconception that we should always be breathing with our belly, but that's just not true. You don't have to do deep breathing constantly, and there's no benefit to it. The point of this exercise is that breathing deeply stimulates the vagus nerve, which relaxes you (Sampson, 2017). This can counteract the feeling of anxiety and make you feel less stressed.

Moving Forward

You might notice that your anxiety is stronger at certain times more than others. This is totally normal! Refer back to these techniques any time that you need them. Over time, you'll learn which ones help you the most.

Combining these techniques with other forms of self-care, like going out for a walk or planning ahead, will make them even more effective. If anxiety is an ongoing struggle and these techniques don't give you relief, speak to your doctor or a licensed therapist. Anxiety is a common experience, and you deserve to feel better!

NOT MAKING PROGRESS

Do you feel like you're working hard and not getting anywhere? Did you miss your goal deadline?

It's normal to have productive times interspersed with periods of rest. Be real with yourself for a second: Are you being overly hard on yourself? Are you expecting to be completely transformed in just a few months or to get through a big life change before you're ready?

If you are, please find some compassion for yourself. What have you accomplished so far? It might seem like nothing, but it's progress that you should celebrate.

You might feel like you're not making any progress, but you're probably doing better than you think. Taking inventory of what you've done so far is a good way to check that!

If you genuinely haven't gotten very far, that's nothing to be ashamed of. Take it as an opportunity to look inward. What's been going on in your life lately? Have you been busy with something unexpected, or have you been dealing with grief or a major life stress?

There are lots of reasons you might not have met your goal, and they aren't all on you. If you're going through something like this, there's no shame in putting your goal on hold until you have the time and headspace to keep going. Write a new check-in date on your calendar and see how you're feeling on that date. Are you ready to start again, or do you need more time? Move at your own pace and be kind to yourself.

If that isn't you, something else is holding you back. To figure out what it is, you need to think about how your goal makes you feel.

When you think about working on your goal, do you feel excited? Terrified? Overwhelmed with existential dread? Try to pinpoint the exact emotions and bodily sensations that come with your goal. Are you tense and achy or stressed out?

Whatever it is for you, have some empathy for yourself. How does it feel to deal with that roadblock? We often don't make progress because we're scared that we won't live up to expectations. Fear can be paralyzing! Before you know it, the deadline has passed, and you haven't even started.

Listen: You aren't lazy, and you aren't a failure! There's always a reason that you aren't making progress. You have to find out what it is and work through it.

After all, it makes sense to work toward stuff that you want. You know that your goal will improve your life exponentially. If it wasn't going to make you happy, you wouldn't have put it into your plan!

When you aren't making progress, you know for sure that something is holding you back. If it's something that you can control, tackle it! Here are the most common reasons that you might be stuck and how to fix them:

- "I won't make it.": You might feel like your efforts will just go to waste, and you won't be able to succeed anyway. This is negative self-talk! If you feel like you can't achieve your goal, you can do two things to feel better. First, break your goal into smaller pieces, so it's not as overwhelming. Second, practice positive or neutral self-talk. You are more capable than you think, and you can do this. You just need to be brave enough to try.

- "I'll just embarrass myself.": You might think that other people won't understand you, or you'll look bad in front of them. The solution here is to stop caring what other people think. I know that this is easier said than done, but how often do you think about how embarrassing other people are? Hopefully never, right? That's how often they think negatively about you. Everyone is busy being the main character of their own story. You deserve to do the same thing! It can help to stop judging people yourself. You might be extremely hard on yourself or other people in your life, so you expect the same from others. If you stop doing that, you'll probably feel less judged in the process.

These worries are deeply tied to the negative narratives and beliefs that we're moving away from. They tend to rear their ugly heads when we push them away. If you want, take another look at Chapter 2 to refresh your memory on them.

Dealing with these feelings is crucial to make the changes you crave. It's okay if it's a slow process. Just be kind and gentle with yourself.

Why Motivation Doesn't Work (and What to Do Instead)

If you're wondering why your motivation peters out before you've achieved your goal, here's why: *It's supposed to.* Motivation isn't supposed to be the only thing fueling you. It's a feeling—just like feeling inspired or excited. It might be a feeling that makes work easier, but it shouldn't be your main source of energy.

You don't get up and go to your job every day because you feel motivated. You do it because it's just what you do. That's kind of magical, isn't it? When things become habitual, they stop being so hard. We do them on autopilot.

That's what you want to do with your goals, especially if you're having a hard time with them. You want to make them so easy and habitual that you don't have to think about them. They just happen for you.

Here's how you do that.

Habit Stacking

If you want to work toward your goal without even trying, try making a habit stack. Take a habit that you already have, like your morning coffee, and add your new habit onto that. For example, you might draw a little doodle while drinking your morning coffee every day. This could be a great way to slowly improve your art skills.

This works because it gives you a trigger that reminds you to work toward your goal. After you do this a few times, it'll start to feel weird when you *don't* do that little activity alongside your old habit.

Make It Easy

I know you want to make big, mind-blowing progress. You're going to get there! For now, though, you want to keep things as simple as possible. You want the work you do toward your goal to be so easy that it would be ridiculous *not* to do it.

You want to make it easier to work on your goal than any other task. You want it to be easy to write 50 words and super hard to check social media. You can do that by setting up your environment to match. For example, when you get home from work, you can put your phone across the room to charge and plop yourself at your desk in front of a document. As soon as you write those 50 words, you're free to do whatever you want. Not doing it seems almost embarrassing when it's such a small task, especially when you know how much you want to meet your goal. Plus, your phone is all the way over *there...*

By making the task you want to complete the easiest, you'll end up doing it automatically. Over time, it will become a habit that you don't have to think about.

Slowly Add On

Once you're consistently meeting your daily goals, you can up the ante a little. Add on a little more, but don't go crazy with it! You want to increase enough that you're on track to meet your deadline. Remember that you can move the deadline if you're not making progress fast enough but do try to meet it!

EXCESSIVE SHAME

You might be anxious or not making progress because you feel unworthy of a better life. This can show up in a few different ways.

Feeling Like a Burden

Are you afraid to change your life because you don't want to burden others? You might want to be less of a doormat but feel guilty about being less available to your friends.

Feeling like a burden keeps you from being honest about your needs. It ties in with perfectionism, because you feel like you have to be perfect to be worthy of another person's love and attention. That's not true!

When you're worried about burdening others, you're putting their convenience over your well-being. You're deciding that it's more worthwhile to feel crappy than to take five minutes out of someone's day.

It doesn't make sense, right? So, whenever you feel the urge to isolate yourself or stay the same for others, think about your priority list. Why are you putting yourself at the bottom again? You deserve better than that!

Unworthiness

Maybe you need to buy certain materials to learn about your passions, but you feel unworthy of the cost. This is a common way for shame to manifest. You might only buy the bare necessities because you feel ashamed of spending money on yourself.

That's your hard-earned cash! If you need to hear this today, it is okay to spend money on yourself. It's okay to splurge sometimes. Think about investing in your hobbies like investing in yourself and your future. You're spending money now so that you can try something fun.

These feelings of shame are keeping you from making progress just like anxiety does, so you can use the same techniques to deal with it. Personification is a great strategy! You can use it to recognize where your feelings are coming from to make them less overwhelming. Like anxiety, it's a learned behavior that is trying to protect you.

Feeling ashamed is supposed to help you get along better in groups. Shame makes you feel bad when you do something that hurts other people, so you don't do it again. When you feel ashamed of yourself as a person, that isn't so helpful. Like we discussed in Chapter 2, that's *toxic shame*. It makes you feel like you don't deserve good things, or you can't get better.

Well, you can!

To deal with lingering toxic shame, you need to create a positive narrative and do positive self-talk. Instead of tearing yourself down, you need to build yourself up. Reaffirm that you are a good person who deserves this positive life change.

Practice small acts of kindness on yourself. Do something nice for yourself, like splurging on your favorite coffee, doing a meditation, or giving yourself a neck massage. These little things build up over time to teach you that you're worthy of good treatment and self-love.

RELATIONSHIP STRAIN

Another reason that you might feel stressed out is relationship strain. As you make progress in your life, you might notice new tensions in your relationships.

Any time you're making a big change in your life, it will also be an adjustment for the people who are close to you. They have to get used to a version of you that is a little bit different than before. Depending on how good your friends and family are with change, this can be difficult.

Communicate!

Tell your loved ones about the changes that you're making. They should be proud of you for making such a big positive difference in your life! Plus, knowing what you're going through will make them more understanding.

If they aren't supportive, they might have their reasons. Being open to the thoughts and concerns of your loved ones is great. They could have some great suggestions or questions for you that you haven't thought of. They should have your best interests at heart, so consider their perspective before you do anything drastic.

That being said, not everyone is a great friend. Some people might be jealous of your progress or are used to walking all over you. If part of your plan is to be less of a doormat, that might not work for your narcissistic friend. If you get the vibe that someone is purposely misunderstanding you or making your life difficult because you're making a change, it might be time to reevaluate.

Reevaluating Relationships

When you feel like a friend might be using you, it's normal to feel betrayed. It can be hard to realize that someone only wanted to be close to you because you did so much for them. Remember that losing them is a win for you because you'll have more free time for the friends who actually care about you.

If you aren't sure if it's time to go, here are some questions to consider:

- Does this person's presence make me feel better or worse?
- Do they hold my values and respect my boundaries?
- Do they seem to genuinely care about me?
- Would losing them as a friend make me sad or relieved?

After answering these questions honestly, you'll know if it's time to leave them behind.

If relationship strain is stressing you out, there's some good news. While it's common to have some tension as you adjust to a new stage in your life, it doesn't tend to stick around. Relationship strain might mean that some friends are becoming closer, while others are moving further away. You might be getting a few open slots to fill with friends that will make you happier. When you've finished this transition period, you'll come out the other side feeling way better.

A BADASS CHECK-IN

A lot of old demons can rear their heads when we start really trying to improve our lives. In times like these, anxiety, shame, and stress can run rampant. It's so important to keep being kind to yourself and remember who you are. You're not the kind of person who lets these feelings get the better of you.

You're a badass! You're smart, tough, and you know exactly what you want. These feelings might shake you up a little, but they can't pull you under. You can do this!

11

HOW TO KNOW WHEN YOU'VE MADE IT

You've been making tons of changes to try and improve your life, but it can be hard to tell if they're working for you. Progress isn't always linear, and it might feel like your goals are still out of reach. How do you know if you're making the right changes for you?

There are some pretty obvious signs that you're thriving and embracing your inner badass. It might take some time for them to become habits, but noticing them off and on is still a great sign. It means that you're on a path that really honors you!

DOING STUFF YOU LIKE

Before you made any changes, you probably spent most of your time vegging out. Scrolling endlessly on social media and binge-watching TV were your jam.

You'll know that you're making progress when you find yourself doing activities that you enjoy instead of just checking your phone obsessively. You might be cooking more, getting outside, or reading before bed. Maybe you play hockey once a week. Cool!

The key here is baby steps. You want to spend less time doing addicting, habitual behaviors (like checking your socials) and more time engaging with hobbies and loved ones. You can't go from being glued to your phone to throwing it in the trash, and you wouldn't want to. Finding little ways to insert more joy into your life is all that matters.

Making Social Media Fun Again

Now, I don't mean that you can't like scrolling through social media or watching shows. Of course you can! Both of those things can be part of a healthy, happy life.

So many of us just use social media as a comparison tool. You might follow lots of models or clothing brands that make you feel bad about your body. You might watch TV shows that you don't really like (or that you've seen a million times) just to fill the silence. You want to make the way you use media more satisfying and mindful.

Unfollow accounts that make you feel bad and stop watching shows that don't excite you just to fill the silence. Instead, spend a minute curating a social media feed that inspires you to be your most authentic self. Watch shows that help you learn, grow, or just have a great time.

Be mindful about what you let into your world. Why expose yourself to draining content that makes you feel worse?

Being mindful doesn't mean you can't watch that show you adore for the umpteenth time or spend four hours on your phone on a Saturday. It just means that you're choosing those behaviors because they make you happy—not doing them out of habit.

Making social media empowering only adds to your life. Plus, this means more time being present, reading, and looking at stuff that makes you feel good rather than numbly scrolling.

When Numb Is Okay

Like most of us, you might notice that you're more vegetative after a rough day. When you begin feeling burnout, the last thing you want is to do more work—even if it's for yourself. You just want to stop for a while.

That's understandable and healthy. When you have a particularly rough day and need to turn your brain off for an hour, there's nothing wrong with flopping in front of the TV. It can feel good to just let go.

Try to choose activities that will help you the most. For example, you might feel better if you take a warm bath and read than if you watch *Jeopardy!* reruns until midnight. It's all about choosing an activity that will be the most comforting and helpful for you at that moment.

Sometimes, you have to consider how much willpower you have to begin with. If you're running on empty, the concept of running the bath, finding a clean towel, and getting undressed can sound like a little much. What you need at that moment might be to just sit in front of the TV or lay down for a nap.

Give yourself permission to relax when you need to, and don't feel bad about it. As you work toward doing more things that you like, you'll probably spend less time doing stuff like this, so you have even less reason to resent spending some time relaxing. Don't expect perfection from yourself.

RELATIONSHIP SATISFACTION

As you discovered in the last chapter, making big changes in your life can cause upheaval in your relationships. As you continue to grow, that upheaval shouldn't stick around. You should find yourself having better quality friendships with people you like to hang out with.

You might find yourself being more vulnerable with the people in your life, which creates closeness and connection.

On the other hand, you might notice that you have fewer poor-quality friendships. If your life was full of leeching frenemies and unhealthy connections, having less of those is still a good sign. Sometimes, you have to lose some before you gain. In this case, though, you're releasing connections that weren't making you happy anyway. Making more time for yourself is a benefit in itself.

As you build your relationship with yourself, you'll require higher quality friends to compete with your alone time. It won't be worthwhile for you to entertain friends that make you feel bad because you could have a way better time by yourself.

If you were one of those people that used to be terrified to be alone, enjoying your own company is a big deal. You'll notice yourself being more selective about friends, which is a huge sign of improvement!

Alternatively, noticing vulnerability and one or two close connections is a huge deal for isolating types. You don't need to have a million friends to improve your life. Just one or two can make all the difference.

Your Relationship With Yourself

Your relationship with others is deeply connected to your relationship with yourself. As your experiences with other people improve, your relationship with yourself should flourish, too.

You might notice that you enjoy spending time alone and feel less judgmental toward yourself. You might catch yourself before something negative even comes to mind and replace it with a positive thought. Your mind is becoming less stressful and more peaceful.

Over time, you'll start picking up activities or habits that you do alone. It might be a nightly walk, a weekly coffee run, or a trip to the beach. Enjoying doing things by yourself *and* with other people is a huge sign that you're feeling better and improving.

It might be harder to judge your progress with yourself if you're used to spending time alone. Keep in mind how you feel when you're alone and how often you're reaching out to other people. If you're keeping in contact with people you love and feeling happy about your alone time, that's great! In general, loneliness and unhappiness should dissipate over time as you make more positive changes. As always, speak with your primary care doctor if they don't.

PROGRESS

Take a look at all the progress you've made so far. You've gone from trying items on a possibility list to making your dreams happen! You should be proud of how far along you are—even if you haven't met your goals yet. They're works in progress now instead of blank canvases, and that's something to celebrate.

Any movement toward your goal is positive. If you're making less progress than you thought, think about why that's happening. Take another look at Chapter 10 if you're feeling stuck but remember: Progress toward your goals isn't the only way to measure improvement.

You might be making progress in your mindset by being less rigid and demanding of yourself. Maybe you're making progress in finding satisfying friendships, and you've been so busy that you haven't gotten around to your other goals yet.

That's totally fine. No one's expecting you to achieve everything in one night!

This whole process is about self-compassion and development.

Changing Goals

You might realize that the goal you set last month isn't what you want after all. That's growth, baby!

Realizing you spent all this time and energy on a goal that you don't care about anymore can be demoralizing. Why set a new goal when the old one didn't work out?

Recognizing that your goal isn't speaking to you is a sign of progress and self-development. To do that, you have to do two major things that most people have trouble with: admitting that you made a mistake and being honest with yourself.

It isn't easy to admit that you wasted your time to yourself or to anyone else. You have to admit that you chose wrong. You picked something that isn't working out for you and doesn't mesh with what you want anymore. Being willing to notice that and adapt to create a new goal is an incredible skill.

It would be so much easier to lie to yourself and pretend that you're happy. We all have experience with that. Too many people decide they want to make a career change only to realize they didn't find the right one yet. Instead of trying again and finding something new, they might stick with what isn't making them happy because they don't want to try again. This seems easier because you don't have to change anything. In the long term, though, this involves way more suffering.

Being brave enough to admit you messed up and try again is huge. It means that you've changed and grown enough to see something in yourself that you couldn't see before.

It doesn't mean that you've failed. It just means that you're learning.

If you're wondering if it's time to give up on an old goal, here are some telltale signs:

- Working on it doesn't make you happy.
- You feel resentful about the choice you made.
- Something came up that excites you more.

You'll know in your heart if it's time to move on. If it is, don't be ashamed of that! Be proud that you've learned so much about yourself. You're one step closer to your best life.

When setting a new goal, you want to keep a few things in mind:

- What made the old goal exciting (at first)?
- What made it bad in the long run?
- What excites me now?
- Will this goal appeal to me in the long term?
- How can I keep it exciting?

Keep learning, growing, and getting to know yourself better. You'll get where you want to be.

FEELING BETTER!

Yes, it's great to meet your goals and make good friends, but the most important thing is that you come out the other side feeling better about your life. If the changes you've made are making you happier, you're on the right track—regardless of anything else.

That's right: This is the ultimate indicator of positive change. It doesn't matter if you've failed to meet all of your goals. It doesn't matter if you've only lost friends since you started. The *only* thing that really matters is if you're feeling better than you were before.

Obviously, there are degrees of feeling better. Cutting out a toxic friend might make you feel 8% better, and quitting your awful job might make you feel 20% better. That's still only 28% better, so we've got some room to grow. Plus, you can feel 300%

better than you did before. It all depends on how awful you felt and how much you can improve your life, so take time to celebrate every single percentage.

Keep this in mind, though: You'll probably never feel 100% perfect. There will always be something going on that keeps it from being the perfect life—even if you do everything you can to improve it. The goal isn't to get to 100% perfection. The goal is to get above 50%. At that point, you just want to be optimistic about the rest.

A Nice(r) Inner Voice

Have you gone from beating yourself up to treating yourself like a human being? That's awesome!

I'm not expecting you to pat yourself on the back every time you do a good job, so it's okay if you aren't there yet. If you respect yourself enough to avoid self-defeating thoughts, you've made it.

Keep being kind to yourself and rewriting that inner narrative. Changing your story from hateful to neutral is a huge deal, and it's something you should be proud of. As you keep working at it, you'll eventually move into positive territory. Slow progress is still progress!

Confidence

You'll know that you've made it when you feel comfortable being yourself around other people. You don't worry about what other people think of you quite so much. You don't need everyone in the room to like you. You're happy just to be yourself. That's something to strive for!

Less Ruminating, Anxiety, and Shame

On a similar note, you shouldn't feel as much anxiety and shame as before. They might still be there, but they should be less aggressive and easier to manage. That's partly because of all the work you've done to improve your self-perception and reduce negative narrative. You're starting to tell a different story about yourself, and it shows!

When negative feelings do come up, it's easier for you to handle them because you have so many helpful coping strategies under your belt. You can use the 5-4-3-2-1 technique to calm yourself in a pinch, and you can combat shame with positive self-talk.

You should find yourself ruminating less about your past and feeling less anxious about the future, too.

Life Satisfaction

You should feel less like life is kicking your ass and more like you're doing the kicking. Major aspects of your life should be falling gradually into place. You might have figured out where you want to live or where you really don't. Maybe you've found an exciting new job or figured out a little more about what you value. The outcomes might not be obvious yet, but some major pieces are shifting around in a way that feels better and truer to who you are.

In general, you should feel happier with your circumstances and yourself. That's when you know you've made some incredible progress.

A BADASS CHECK-IN

As you worked through this book, you should've noticed your confidence and happiness slowly going up. You should be enjoying life more overall in a bunch of small ways. The negatives should have gone way down, with things like stress, anxiety, and fear having less of an impact. Instead, self-love, hobbies, and positive relationships should be taking up their space. It probably isn't perfect yet, but I hope you can feel that you've taken a step in a happier direction.

You've worked really hard to uncover your inner badass, and what you've learned about yourself can't be undone by anyone else. When you start to see your worth, you never settle for less! You're a powerful, kind, and smart woman with an amazing future ahead of you. Never forget it!

CONCLUSION

You've made so much progress on your quest for a happier, more fulfilling life! This transformation has helped you reconnect with your true self and rediscover your self-confidence. You've truly embraced your inner badass!

When you started out, you were a powerful woman in a major rut. You made choices that didn't feel like your own, felt trapped in routine, and settled for things that didn't make you happy. You knew deep down that you deserved better, but you weren't sure how to get there.

You started recognizing your negative thought patterns, the story you believe about your life, and how you grapple with societal expectations. You realized that it isn't always you against the world. In a lot of ways, you're harder on yourself than anyone else has been. By paying attention to these behaviors, you've slowly rewritten the narrative in your head. Even if you aren't necessarily your own best friend, you can respect and value yourself as a human being. That's such an incredible change! You're not willing to let other people control your future anymore because you know your own worth.

In Chapter 3, you unpacked where these negative self-beliefs came from. Learning about your childhood and where you picked up these behaviors was eye-opening for sure. You discovered that these negative beliefs helped you when you were growing up and that's why they're so hard to get rid of now. This made you more understanding of yourself, so you could be more empathetic on your journey. Since then, you've started to have your own back.

Then, you learned that the way you talk to yourself impacts more than your mind: It hurts your body, too. To fully heal, you need to take care of your body and your brain. That doesn't mean going on a diet or taking up running; it just means paying attention to how your body feels and doing things that make you feel good in the long run. Ultimately, fostering a kind relationship with your body and your mind is key. You started listening to your body and respecting it rather than hating it. It might not be love yet, but it's definitely a step in the right direction!

In Chapter 5, you did some deep digging into your behavior. You learned which attachment style you have and how it's been impacting your relationships. This discovery helped you better understand where people with other attachment styles are coming from, reducing the strain in your relationships. All attachment styles are ways of handling stress or uncertainty in our relationships, so fixing them is about learning to trust. Being vulnerable with yourself and others is difficult, but it'll be worth it in the long run. You realized that being real with other people is the only way to get what you want, and it opens the door to real communication and connection.

You also learned to value your own time and energy. You saw the impact that bad friends can have on your life and stopped putting up with people who only make you feel worse. Go you!

That ties in with what you did in Chapter 6: You finally shut up the voice in your head that says you aren't good enough. Slowly but surely, you've been improving the way you talk to yourself.

Learning to express and release your emotions through exercise, writing, and other methods was a huge source of relief, too. You learned all about effective self-compassion and the benefits of reparenting. You started to dedicate time and space to your own healing.

At this point, you started thinking about the future. You built a solid understanding of where your behaviors came from and how they were affecting you so you could decide what needed to change. Then, you started figuring out how positive change would look for you. What would be included, and what had to go? You thought long and hard about what you want before you started trying stuff that might work.

You experimented to find out what suited you moving forward, and you might have gotten different results than you first expected. Sorting through all of your passions, you narrowed down to the ones that make you the happiest and that you're most eager to spend time on. Little by little, you wrote out the future you wanted. It took courage to put yourself out there, but it helped you figure out what's right for you.

Making it happen is a whole other story, and that part might still be in progress. It's challenging to make big changes in your life, and you learned techniques in Chapter 10 to keep you grounded through this transformational period. Things might not be exactly how you want them, but you're getting there little by little.

Throughout the whole process, you've learned to have faith in yourself. You're capable of so much more than you thought. You're a force to be reckoned with!

You've already made a huge change in your life just by reading this book. You've collected so much information about who you are and who you want to be and used it to rewrite your future. When you started this journey, you felt stuck and unsure. You might've repressed what you wanted just to keep the status quo.

Look how far you've come! You've worked through the stuff that kept you down to transform into your most authentic, badass self. You're not afraid to be bold and stand up for what you believe in, because you know exactly who you are and what you want. Embracing possibility didn't leave you vulnerable or lost like you first thought it would. Instead, it helped you realize who you really are. And you're a total badass!

So... why stop now? You've come a long way, but you've still got a few tweaks to make as you work toward your ideal life. You can refer back to this book any moment you need comfort, motivation, or advice. Keep being kind and loving toward yourself; keep moving forward!

At the end of the day, you know what's inside you. You know how fierce, determined, and lovable you are. You deserve the world, so get out there and make it yours!

Use the QR code to get your copy of the free companion workbook or go to https://dl.bookfunnel.com/hb8r3frj1l.

REFERENCES

Cárthaigh, S. M., Griffin, C., & Perry, J. (2020). The relationship between sleep and problematic smartphone use among adolescents: A systematic review. *Developmental Review, 55,* 100897. https://doi.org/10.1016/j.dr.2020.100897

Chu, M. (2017, September 12). *This researcher reveals how lucky people differ from unlucky people.* Inc.com. https://www.inc.com/melissa-chu/want-to-become-luckier-heres-what-you-need-to-do-a.html

Cleave, I. (2021, May 6). *Why you should be a badass woman.* BARE Dating: Meet, Date, Repeat. https://bare.dating/tips-and-advice/why-you-should-be-a-bad-ass-woman

Dye, H. (2018). The impact and long-term effects of childhood trauma. *Journal of Human Behavior in the Social Environment, 28*(3), 381–392. https://doi.org/10.1080/10911359.2018.1435328

Firth, J., Siddiqi, N., Koyanagi, A., Siskind, D., Rosenbaum, S., Galletly, C., Allan, S., Caneo, C., Carney, R., Carvalho, A. F., Chatterton, M. L., Correll, C. U., Curtis, J., Gaughran, F., Heald, A., Hoare, E., Jackson, S. E., Kisely, S., Lovell, K., & Maj, M. (2019). The Lancet Psychiatry Commission: a blueprint for protecting physical health in people with mental illness. *The Lancet Psychiatry, 6*(8), 675–712. https://doi.org/10.1016/s2215-0366(19)30132-4

Ganley, C. (2018, August 14). *Are boys better than girls at math?* Scientific American. https://www.scientificamerican.com/article/are-boys-better-than-girls-at-math/

Hasan, S. (2018). *Posttraumatic stress disorder (for teens).* KidsHealth. https://kidshealth.org/en/teens/ptsd.html

Helm, P. J., Jimenez, T., Bultmann, M., Lifshin, U., Greenberg, J., & Arndt, J. (2020). Existential isolation, loneliness, and attachment in young adults. *Personality and Individual Differences, 159,* 109890. https://doi.org/10.1016/j.paid.2020.109890

Kansky, J. (2018). What's love got to do with it? Romantic relationships and well-being. In E. Diener, S. Oishi, & L. Tay (Eds.), *Handbook of well-being.* DEF Publishers.

Levitt, S. D. (2020). Heads or tails: The impact of a coin toss on major life decisions and subsequent happiness. *The Review of Economic Studies, 88*(1), 378–405. https://doi.org/10.1093/restud/rdaa016

Lucas, G. (2018). Gut thinking: The gut microbiome and mental health beyond the head. *Microbial Ecology in Health and Disease, 29*(2). https://doi.org10.1080/16512235.2018.1548250

Majer, M., Nater, U. M., Lin, J.-M. S., Capuron, L., & Reeves, W. C. (2010). Association of childhood trauma with cognitive function in healthy adults: A pilot study. *BMC Neurology, 10*(1). https://doi.org/10.1186/1471-2377-10-61

Malan-Muller, S., Valles-Colomer, M., Raes, J., Lowry, C. A., Seedat, S., & Hemmings, S. M. J. (2018). The gut microbiome and mental health: Implications for anxiety- and trauma-related disorders. *OMICS: A Journal of Integrative Biology, 22*(2), 90–107. https://doi.org/10.1089/omi.2017.0077

Mind. (2021, January). *What is complex PTSD?* https://www.mind.org.uk/information-support/types-of-mental-health-problems/post-traumatic-stress-disorder-ptsd-and-complex-ptsd/complex-ptsd/

Mitchell, A. (2018, June 29). *The 12 areas of life balance.* The Design Coach. https://www.thedesigncoach.com.au/post/the-12-areas-of-life-balance

Raimondi, G. (2019, August 26). *On insecure avoidant (dismissive & fearful) attachment styles.* http://gwynnraimondi.com/on-insecure-avoidant-dismissive-fearful-attachment-styles/

Robson, D., & Gray, R. (2007). Serious mental illness and physical health problems: A discussion paper. *International Journal of Nursing Studies, 44*(3), 457–466. https://doi.org/10.1016/j.ijnurstu.2006.07.013

Sampson, S. (2017, June 28). *Vagus nerve: Function, stimulation, and further research.* Medical News Today. https://www.medicalnewstoday.com/articles/318128#What-is-the-vagus-nerve

Selva, J. (2018, January 5). *How to set healthy boundaries: 10 examples + PDF worksheets*. PositivePsychology.com. https://positivepsychology.com/great-self-care-setting-healthy-boundaries/

Smith, S. (2018, April 10). *5-4-3-2-1 coping technique for anxiety*. Www.urmc.rochester.edu. https://www.urmc.rochester.edu/behavioral-health-partners/bhp-blog/april-2018/5-4-3-2-1-coping-technique-for-anxiety.aspx

Spence, R., Jacobs, C., & Bifulco, A. (2018). Attachment style, loneliness and depression in older age women. *Aging & Mental Health, 24*(5), 837–839. https://doi.org/10.1080/13607863.2018.1553141

Suni, E. (2020, August 14). *What is sleep hygiene?* Sleep Foundation. https://www.sleepfoundation.org/sleep-hygiene

Sussman, C. (2021). Escape from the escape: Addressing screen media in individual psychotherapy. *Journal of the American Academy of Child and Adolescent Psychiatry, 60*(10), S39. https://pesquisa.bvsalud.org/global-literature-on-novel-coronavirus-2019-ncov/resource/pt/covidwho-1466455

The Attachment Project. (2020, July 2). *Anxious attachment: Causes & symptoms*. Attachment Project. https://www.attachmentproject.com/blog/anxious-attachment/

ABOUT THE AUTHOR

Olivia Kimble is an integrative healing specialist focused on using psychology, wellness, and spirituality to help women feel better and become their most authentic selves. She guides women to uncover the negative thoughts and self-perceptions that keep them feeling stuck, so they can finally pursue a more fulfilling life. Olivia garnered a personal understanding of these issues through her own lived experience. Initially starting off in interior design, Olivia came to realize her passion for women's wellness. She began a new career as a certified lymphatic therapist and Emotion Code practitioner where she worked one-on-one to support clients' emotional and physical health. This helped her to develop a keen understanding of the brain-body connection. She has since shifted her entrepreneurial passions into writing, so she can support, motivate, and inspire other women while traveling the world, staying true to her own possibility list!

Her fascination with people and places expands to all areas of the globe. She has been to 96 countries so far but keeps finding more to explore. She has always been fascinated with culture and tradition, as it shows the ways of knowing ourselves and each other. She believes that learning about the world and our many differences only shows how much we have in common. When she isn't writing or traveling, you can find Olivia spending time with her friends and family, painting, enjoying art, and cooking. She also adores her rescue cats and exploring the great outdoors. She lives in Hawaii and has two young adult children.

Made in the USA
Middletown, DE
17 March 2023

26950366R00080